"...stays true to his music by making MCs su[...]
— **The Source M**[...]

"Real T@lk's words are familiar like the great poets of the past - Brooks, Hughes & Angelou, but refreshing like the 808s in hip-hop. He covers a range of topics - love, social issues & more from his unique perspective in a way that forces you to reflect on your own experiences. He is truly a poet of the people!"
— **Donnie Smith**
Executive Director of **Donda's House Inc.**

"His work is unique, profound, and very contemporary."
— **Preston Jackson**
Professor Emeritus, the Art Institute of Chicago

"Jedi rap shit at its finest."
— **Big Boi**, OutKast

"True words of wisdom that cut deep into hearts. Words that open minds. Words of power!"
— **Apollonia**

"Real T@lk opens doors for the ancestors, women and men who need to heal their wounded perceptions about love, relationships and family...he provides a requiem for love for those who confuse it for lust, disrespect and bastardized nouns."
— **Ayesha Jaco**
co-founder/Executive Director of The Lupe Fiasco Foundation

"Real T@lk teaches us pro verbs to escape these death sentences."
— **Ray Murray**
co-founder, Organized Noize Productions

"Real T@lk has magic in his words. He's a beast with the wordplay. The perspective of his stories is unique, powerful, and life-changing."
— **J. Ivy**
award-winning poet and author

"If you've ever seen him on stage, you know how he makes you want to see his words on the page. In these pages, you'll be directed right back to the stage, wanting to hear them again. It's a window into the work space of lyrical mastery. This work is the epitome of Real T@lk."
— **A.D. Carson, PhD**

emcee, educator, and author of *COLD* and *The City*
"Grossly underrated, remains one of the sickest lyricists repping Chicago.
You snooze, you lose."
— **GY312**, Genius.com

"I've honestly witnessed the growth of this dude's amazing career and
I'm proud to say he's one of the most gifted artists to ever come out of Chicago."
— **Lil Rel Howery**,
comedian, actor and writer

"An elite wordsmith. You'd be hard–pressed to find an emcee with his precision
and creativity when it comes to writing and delivery."
— **K. Love**
national spoken word artist, founder of L.Y.R.I.C. Mentoring

(she calls me) mr.write

AN ANTHOLOGY.

brandon alexander williams

Printed in the United States of America First Printing, 2016

ISBN: 1-7908280-3-6
ISBN-13: 978-1-7908280-3-6

Cover Art Photography: Brian Freeman
Editorial Consultant: A.D. Carson, PhD

brandon alexander williams

for my contemporaries:

ignore it if you think it's wack.
support it if it's dope,
and just leave it at that.

reserve your energy.

contents

This is dedicated to *Nabi's House* and the Chicago poetry scene.

d.c. is definitely ready for us, b! (*cam'ron voice*)

After a few years of performing around the Illinois, St. Louis, Indiana and Ohio college circuit, I decided to hit up Washington D.C. I recall several poets talking about hitting up D.C., mentioning Busboys and Poets. D.C. this, D.C. that! So I said to myself, "Let me find out what all of the hoopla is about."

I type in my address bar: "maps.google.com" and open several other tabs for Facebook, Gmail, Megabus, Greyhound, Amtrak and Google (*a ritual while contemplating spitting in unfamiliar territory.*) I post a status on Facebook then copy and paste, "I wonder who I know in the DMV..."

(*Typing on computer in travel agent mode.*)
Voice in my head: Washington D.C. Howard. Georgetown. Lemme see who I know in D.C. Matt, from NIU? I thought he was in Chicago. Howard University Film School? That's dope.
(*Sends Matt a message. Receives an instant message from Fontane*)
Fontane: MAB, you know Rich is in DC
Me: Word? I'll try and hit him up.
(*A comment posts on my status.*)
Person on Facebook: Candace Griffin is there! She works for BET.
Voice in my head: Dope. I'll definitely hit her up. She's the homie.
(*Clicks on Google tab*) Busboys and poets...(*Clicks link*) fifth and K, 14th and V, Hyattsville, Arlington-Shirlington...
(*Flips through cell contacts. Stops. Dials "X St. Louis"*)
X: B, what's up Fam?
Me: Yo, I keep hearing dope things about D.C. I'm thinking about going. I know you travel a lot, do you know any poets or hosts there?
X: Aww yeah, that's a great market. They'll love you too. Especially with your style, they'll catch the bars. And they'll buy product so make sure you bring plenty of CDs.
Me: okay okay, bet!
(*Clicks on Megabus tab*)
Voice in my head: I wonder if there's a Megabus from Chicago to Washington D.C.
(*Clicks on Greyhound tab*)
Voice in my head: Watch this be like a hundred dollars...20hours?!

Hell naw.

X: It's pretty easy to get around the city.

(*Google searches: "DC public transportation". Clicks on "Metro"*)

X: Oh! You gotta hit up Droopy, he's Drew Anderson on Facebook. He hosts Spit Dat on Thursdays. That's a weekly joint. Umm Wednesday is "Verses" at Bohemian Caverns.

(*Opens a blank Word document*)

Me: Who did what now?

X: Bohemian Caverns.

Me: Bohemian like Rhapsody...Wayne's World. Cavern like cave?

X: Yeah. Yeah...with an "S"...caverns. A sister by the by the name of Lorna Pinckney hosts that. L-O-R-N-A. Pinckney. Busboys has several locations, just google their website.

Me: (*typing*) Thank you Thank you.

X: Oh yeah, There's a Friday in Baltimore but that's like 45 to an hour away. It's not weekly tho. Matta fact, go to Poetry247.com. Almost every set in the DMV is listed on there.

(*Clicks apple + T. Goes to Poetry247.com*)

Voice in my head: Lemme check this ou...oooh, Jackpot!

Me: aaaaye! Bro thanks. Like for real. This is clutch.

X: No problem.

Voice in my head: We should do this for Chicago

X: Ohhhh wait, there's a small set out in the boondocks. Manassas, Virginia it's called Spirits & Lyrics. Hosted by Simply T.

Me: The letter T or...

X: Tee. T-E-E. She'll prolly set you up for a feature. I'll text you her number.

Me: 'preciate this Fam, for real. I'm Finna set up this trip to DC.

X: Aiight man Peace

Me: Peace.

    I arranged lodging plans between Matt and Candace. After looking at a map of the Midwest, DC, Maryland and Virginia for about an hour, I purchase a one-way Megabus ticket from Chicago to Cleveland, another subsequent Megabus from Cleveland to Pittsburgh, and last (*but not least*) a Greyhound ticket from Pittsburgh to Washington D.C. I board the Megabus with a digital camouflage army duffel bag full of clothes, a gang of Mo' Better Mixtapes, CD inserts, jewel cases, a brain full of poems, raps and a beam of positive energy. I was prepared. I was thirsty for poetry, hip-hop, cyphers...I was ready for all that the District of Columbia, Maryland and Virginia had to offer. I send a text to my homie Tyson before I step on stage at Spit Dat:

Me: "Reporting Live from D.C. I'm finna SNAP!"
Tyson: "I wouldn't expect anything less, Fam."

the outkast story, part one

It all started on my 26th birthday, January 19th, 2012. While visiting my girlfriend, Whitney at Illinois State University I got "The Phone Call" that would change my life forever. I later would learn that this legendary phone call was set into motion by my Whitney with the help of Andre's older cousin Angelo Redding (aka Lo), and her older sister, Portia.

In 2010 or 2011 (I don't recall precisely), Portia's friend "L" (who produced two joints on *The Talented Tenth 8.0 LP*) invited her to an event in Chicago where Big Boi would be. "L" had access to VIP where Portia and him both met Big Boi and "Lo". While leaving the event, Lo told L and Portia that they were cool people and to stay in touch because he and Big's crew we're not "Hollywood". Long story short, they ended up fostering a business relationship. Portia informed me every now and then of what they were working on. A few weeks before my birthday, she told me that Lo was planning an event that would take place in Atlanta, GA and she would need me to DJ.

Now fast-forward to my 26th birthday, Whitney told me that I'd get a call from Portia regarding the aforementioned event in Atlanta. Portia calls me and says that a representative from her company would be calling me to get a price quote for my DJ services. Some random 404 area code number calls me. I decline. Portia calls and informs me that it would be in my best interest to answer any 404 area code numbers that call my phone today.

Me: Hello?
Lo: Is this Brandon Williams...DJ Hollywood?
Me: This is he.
Lo: Okay cool cool. You've been referred by Portia Mittons to DJ our launch in Atlanta, Georgia. How would you feel about coming down here to DJ?
Me: That'll be dope! I've only been to Atlanta once.
Lo: Okay, are you familiar with Southern music? You'll have to play a good amount at this event, this is "the A".
Me: Of course! I'm familiar with the current sound.
Lo: Oh yeah, well who's hot right now?
Me: Well, T.I., Jeezy, 2 Chainz, Gucci, Travis Porter...

Lo: Okay Okay, you know a little bit.

Me: (*interrupting*) Yeah but, I was introduced to hip-hop in the 90s, so as far as hip-hop in Atlanta...OutKast all day! Dungeon Family...

Lo: Yeah Outkast is kinda decent

Me: (*interrupting*) Maaan! I grew up listening to Outkast. André 3000 is my favorite rapper.

Lo: Oh yeah? Hold on...

(*Phone fidgeting followed by brief pause.*)

Voice on phone: Brandon!

Voice in my head: I know this ain't Angelo. You know what'd be crazy? If 3000 was on the other end of this phone.

Me: Hello, I'm still here.

Voice on phone: Brandon, what's up man? Happy Birthday!

Voice in my head: Holy smokes. This *is* André 3000 *and* he just wished me happy birthday.

Me: Oohhhhhhhhh WOOOOOH!!!!! OHHHH MY GOD!!

He laughs. Whitney is laughing as well and smiling. I give her the same look that Detective Alonzo Harris gave after Officer Hoyt said, "I'll do anything you want me to do" in *Training Day*. Then I proceed to give Dré an elevator pitch.

Voice in my head: Brandon, breathe. Just be cool. Talk to him like a human being. Whatever you do, do *not* rap for him.

Me: I'm a huge fan, joe! I'm really not a DJ like that, I'm a rapper, well an emcee! I was featured in *The Source Magazine* as *Unsigned Hype*. You're the reason I started rapping!

André 3000: Thanks man. I'm humbled.

Voice in my head: Fam being hella modest. (*laughs*) I'mma be modest like this when I blow up.

Me: You don't understand...

André 3000: What's up?

Me: Fam...I was a part of the OutKast fan club when I was like ten. On the back of *ATLiens* you guys had an address. I wrote to it. Y'all wrote me back. The letter said "Hootie Hoo" at the top.

Voice in my head: I *know* he remembers this, he has to.

André 3000: Yeah! yeah! We *did* have a fan club...and we *did* put that at the top of our letters. Wow thanks man. I really appreciate genuine folks. I'm humbled.

Voice in my head: He doesn't get it, Fam.

Me: You don't understand.

André 3000: What?

Voice in my head: Gone 'head and spit him that Aquemini verse.

Me: Maaaaaan...

> *My mind warps and bends, floats the wind, count to ten,*
> *meet the twin, André Ben, welcome to the lion's den.*
> *Original skin, many men comprehend,*
> *I extend myself so you go out and tell a friend.*
> *Sin all depends on what you're believing in.*
> *Faith is what you make it, that's the hardest since MC Ren.*
> *Alien can blend, right on in, with your kin.*
> *Look again, cause I swear I spot one every now and then.*
> *It's happenin' again, wish I could tell you when,*
> *André this is André y'all is just gon' have to make amends!*

Voice in my head: Yes, verbatim, and I'm *so* glad you didn't mess that up bro, *and* that you didn't rap him your stuff.

André 3000: YEEEEEEAAAAAHHH! HELL YEAH! Maaaan, I don't even remember that verse!

Me: Word?

Voice in my head: Get outta here, André 3000. This is like one of the greatest rap verses of all time.

André 3000: Thanks man...like, for real, I really appreciate genuine fans...I'm humbled. I can't say that enough.

Me: it's all love.

André 3000: Well man we just wanted to wish you a happy birthday...gotta get back to work... you enjoy your birthday.

Me: Can you do me a favor right quick?

André 3000: What's up?

Me: Can you call me back and leave "happy birthday" on my voicemail. Nobody's going to believe me, plus I'm going to use it as a drop on my mixtape.

André 3000: Nah, I can't really do that because then it gets into different legal boundaries and all that...

Me: Oh, okay that's cool, I understand.

Voice in my head: Damn. Shut it down.

André 3000: I'll tell you what, the next time that you come to Atlanta, get in touch with my cousin and we can hang out.

Voice in my head: This is the best day of your life.

Me: Alright then, bet!

André 3000: Alright then man, you enjoy your birthday.

Me: Alright Peace.

After I got off of the phone, I gave Whitney a huge *Martin* sitcom "gimme love"-with the high pitched voice-hug. Later on, I would find out that she bought a vinyl of *ATLiens* last month and had Portia mail the vinyl to Lo to see if he could get Big and André to autograph it. He told Portia that *not only would they sign it*, but he'd try and get André to call me for my birthday. Lo is the Robert Horry in this entire birthday surprise operation! Post-call, Portia called me back about 15 minutes later:

Portia: Hey, Angelo said Dré doesn't just invite folks to the A like that, and he *is* a man of his word so you should take him up on his offer.
Voice in my head: So...you think after André 3000 personally invited me to Atlanta, that I wasn't going to catch a flight down there and meet up with him? Sheiiiid.

the outkast story, part two

Lo: Have you heard from Dre?
Swiff: I just spoke to him.
Lo: Man, lemme see your phone. (*Dials, places on speaker phone*)
Voice on speakerphone: Swiff, what up?
Voice in my head: Oh snap, It's Dre.
Lo: This ain't Swiff, this is your cousin! Man, I've been trying to call you all day!
Voice on speakerphone: My bad, man I've been busy and…
Lo: (*interrupts*) Well look, I got Brandon here with me, the guy that you wished happy birthday to; I want you to meet him.
Voice on speakerphone: Oh okay cool. Come through.
Lo: Where you at?
Voice on speakerphone: The crib.
Voice in my head: Welp, that's dead. He's probably in for the night…definitely not going to his house.
Lo: Well, you wanna come over to Swiff's or meet us at Stankonia?
Voice on speakerphone: Naw, come through. If he's cool with you, he's cool with me.
Lo: Alright then.
Voice on speakerphone: Peace.
Voice in my head: So this means…

Lo hangs up the phone. Cutmaster Swiff and Lo look at each other perplexed.

Swiff: What'd he just say?
Lo: B, I don't want to make you more nervous than you already are, but Dre doesn't invite anyone to his house unless they're Dungeon family or actual family or close friends. He's very private. He must've felt some positive energy to want to even invite you to his house. (*Swiff nods in agreement.*)

On the surface, I'm Frank Underwood with a subtle smirk. Below the surface, I'm Martin Payne post-lottery triumph.

Voice in my head: (*Martin voice*) Woowoo Woo-Woo!

Lo grabs his keys, tells sister Candace and I to ride with him. Of course, he wouldn't have us trail him. I'm pretty sure that was the most intelligent option. Perfect strangers/fans meet ½ of the Grammy award-winning multi-platinum, legendary duo, OutKast at his home. Even if he did, I'm not a stalker by any means, neither is Candace… I think.

During the ride, Lo is schooling us on Dungeon Family history and the beginning of OutKast; he also hit a few circle routes and U-turns as he joked, "I gotta make sure y'all don't know where we are." I distinctly recall him informing me that Dre has been super low key training and rehearsing for a Jimi Hendrix biopic and that he's been refusing photographs lately, so he advised not to inquire.

After about 30 to 40 minutes of swerving up and down the red hills somewhere around the outskirts of Atlanta, we arrive at a large Mary Swanson, Aspen, Colorado-type house with a Cadillac Escalade in a circular driveway. Candace exits the vehicle and walks around to my side and with the exact smile of Braxton P. Hartnabrig boasting his Cornell alumni status and whispers, "I think I heard him, joe!" I whisper back, "Hey, keep it together, and be cool".

I was probably more excited than she was. I think to myself, this had to be how Yeezy felt when he met Jigga, Dame when he met Uncle Rush or 3000 when he met *Alexander Nevermind* for the first ever time. I mentally coached myself earlier during the ride from Swiff's house.

Voice in my head: Okay Brandon. Don't act star-struck. He is a human being. We are all human beings. Treat him like one. It'll be refreshing. I'm sure folks constantly contact him asking for something and acting awkward. Don't be a weirdo. You're not a weirdo, so acting like that will just bring awkward energy into the atmosphere. No one likes to be around awkward or negative energy. Just be yourself. Pay homage and then engage in convo. If you look at him like a celebrity, he'll look at you like a fan. If you speak to him and respect him like the man he is, he'll speak to and respect you equally.

We approach the door, it opens and there he was! I'm 6'2", so he had to be about 5'10" or 5'11". There stood Possum Aloysius Jenkins, in blue jean overalls, Chuck Taylors, a flannel shirt with the sleeves rolled up, all under a bright orange beanie stuffed with an afro, and electric guitar in hand. He practiced a series of specific riffs until the time we left as he spoke with us.

Dre: Come on in
Lo: What's up mane?
Voice in my head: Be cool, ice cold.
Where Are My Panties? Interlude voices: Ice cold!

They dap up each other and catch up a little bit. Lo points to me and tells Dre that I'm the one he wished happy birthday to last month. He reaches out; I embrace with a genuine, contemporary African man-dap-hug.

Andre: What's up man? I'll never forget that call. We weren't on the phone for 30 seconds and you started rapping me my old stuff. That made me feel good.
Voice in my head: Say something, Fam.
Me: Thank you. Andre. Three thousand.
Voice in my head: No! Brandon, What was that, man?
(*Everyone laughs*)

Me: (*pointing to fireplace*) Hey, what's that written upside down?
Andre: Oh, that's where I wrote She Lives in My Lap.
Voice in my head: Wait…what? That's hella epic.
Lo: What you working on?
Andre: I got John downstairs mixing some stuff for me.
Lo: John Frye?
Andre: Yeah
Lo: Can they come down?
Andre: Come on.

We all head downstairs to the studio. On the surface, I'm Danny Ocean, beneath the surface; I'm the sweat shop workers in the 1978 version of The Wiz, jamming to "Brand New Day" post-defeat of Evilene.

Lo: (*Nudges me, smiling*) How you feel man?

Me: I'm good; I'm just keeping everything smooth.

Lo: Naw man! It's all love in here.

Me: (*on the verge of tears*) Dre.

Andre: What's up?

Me: Bro, you're the reason I ever picked up a pen. Like, who was the first artist that you heard and made you want to rap?

Andre: It had to be LL Cool J, I think.

Me: Well, Elevators was my first introduction to hip-hop. 1996, I was like ten, in my cousin Kris's basement and when I heard the bass line and then "*One for the money, yes sir, two for the show*". I was like, "What is this?!" After switching discs, big brother Steve handed me a case that read *Outkast, ATLiens* in graffiti, comic-style bubble letters. I open the case and see a sketch of a naked melanated woman being showered with the color green. I already loved drawing, but from that day forward, I wanted to rap too. Outkast is the reason I started rhyming.

Andre: Wow. I'm humbled man. Really, I can't say that enough.

Me: I gotta rap something for you though.

Voice in my head: No! Actually, go for it, now's the time.

Andre: Go ahead. Here, have a seat.

He removes a guitar from the engineer's chair by the soundboard and sets it against the wall, sits on the floor Native American-style, slightly tilts his head and says, "Lemme hear you." I spit him my fan favorite piece, *Mr. Write*. During the first half of the poem, I notice he's reacting to my flow and certain punchlines. During the remainder of the poem, he catches on to the extended metaphor and personification and at the end, he stands up, **"Man that is dope!"**

"Thank you, thank you. I got another one." I swear I must've spit him like four or five songs worth of verses with brief pauses between. The coolest part was that he never hit me with the Chappelle Show Wrap-It-Up box.

Andre: You know what? You're like a lyrical scientist. Like, you take something and explain it two or three different ways all in a rap. That's dope. And you do all of this with no instruments, not one?
Me: Yeah.
Andre: That's pretty impressive, man.
Me: Thank you. Andre...three thousand.

Everyone laughs. We chop it up further about music, politics and etc. He tells me how much he dislikes social media and the paparazzi. I play him a few original songs of mine and even went out on a limb and played the re-make/cover of *She Lives in My Lap*.

Someone in the room: Andre, can I get a photo with you?
Andre: (*warm smile*) Naw, not today.
Voice in my head: I'm so glad the ice has been broken on that topic!
Andre: (*to me*) wanna hear something?
Me: Yeah!
Voice in my head: No Andre 3000, I don't want to hear an unreleased song that probably sounds awesome. Psych! Of course I do!
Lo: Play him that 16 joint that you and Ross did!

Andre: Alright. (*searches through music files*) Actually, no, I can't play you that one. It's a feature verse for Ross's album but out of respect for that man's art, I won't play you the song or any part.
Me: I can honor that. That makes sense.
Andre: I'll play you this joint I did with Gorillaz.

He proceeds to play me the 13 minute explicit version of *Do Ya Thing*. I recall it being fast-paced with an electric bass line. It had to be upwards of 160 BPM. He comes in on the joint singing and then spits a verse that matches the tempo and then towards the end, he keeps yelling. It was hilarious. I forgot the story verbatim but it was something along the lines of a conversation where they overheard someone in the studio responding to someone and boasting their greatness in a 2011 Charlie Sheen-esque manner.

While we were listening to the song, Lo pulled Candace out of the room. When she returned, she told me that Lo said he's knows his cousin and he can tell that he's comfortable. Now would be the best time to ask him anything and suggested that I ask him for his email address. About 30 more minutes pass. Lo says it's about time to go because he has to drive us back far west to Swiff's house to pick up Candace's car and then drive south to his home in Henry County.

Me: Hey Dre, do you have any pointers for me as an artist?
Andre: You got a lot of punchlines. You would be really great at…umm
Voice in my head: No. Don't say it.
Andre: Battle rap! Them cats be snapping. You'd kill that.
Voice in my head: Damn. You didn't want to hear that.
Me: Yeah, I wouldn't do that. It's either poetry or music for me.
Andre: Cool. You know, I look at the game like rappers and writers. Wayne is a rapper, Drake is a writer. Big is a rapper, he can rap like crazy. I'm more of a writer. You can rap, you got that part down, but I can tell you're a writer like me. You have a lot of concepts. I think you should take those concepts and write more songs. You can connect with the people better that way.
Me: Thank you. I'll really take that into consideration.
Andre: No prob.
Me: Yo, I got a gift for you.
Andre: Oh yeah?
Me: Yeah, I got these stickers with my logo on them. You can put them on your guitar or laptop or something.
Andre: Aww thanks man. I appreciate the gift.
Me: Hold up, I have one more thing for you.

I reach into my book bag and pull out a print of my full page, December 2009 feature in the *The Source Magazine* for "Unsigned Hype" and I sign it, "To Andre 3000, from Real T@lk." He smiled and chuckled:

Andre: "Thank you man. People don't give me gifts that often."
Me: You're welcome.
Voice in my head: This will be a great Segway into asking him for his email.
Andre: Well, y'all be cool, travel safe.
(Daps and hugs all around the room.)
Me: Hey, well you did say I should write more songs. May I have your email to stay in touch and keep you updated on my progress?
Andre: Sure man, just respect my privacy and don't give it out to anyone.
Voice in my head: This brother is just as cool as I always thought he was. Damn, this is a dope experience.

We exchange emails and Lo drives us back to Swiff's house. On the ride home, I recall Candace breaking the silence as we're driving back to Georgia Tech:

Candace: *(laughing)* G…you know you just swagged on Andre 3000, right?
Me: *(confused)* Huh? What do you mean?
Candace: *(laughing more hysterically)* you gave the man a picture of you and autographed it! Hahaha!
Me: *(joining laughter)* Oh no! I didn't mean it like that!
Candace: I know you didn't mean it to be arrogant, and it's dope that he didn't take it that way. It was like a confident gesture. It was like saying, "I'm up next, be on the lookout." Or "I accept the legacy baton for hip-hop".
Me: Yeah! That was it!
Candace: He's real cool! If it was Jay-Z, he would've been like, "What am I supposed to do with this?" and gave it back or not taken it at all.
Me: Hecky yeah.

the outkast story, part three

July 4th, 2012, I released my fourth project, *Fresh Produce* and the following November I released *The Talented Tenth 8.0 LP*. One particular afternoon that summer, while sitting in my parents' living room, eating Cinnamon Toast Crunch and watching *The Office*, I received a phone call from Angelo informing me that Big Boi was working on his second solo album, *Vicious Lies and Dangerous Rumors:*

Lo: B, See if you can come up with a spoken word piece for an intro or interlude on the album.
Me: Alright cool.
Lo: Can you get to a studio today?
Voice in my head: (*Young Jeezy voice*) Yeeaaahhhh!
Me: Yes, sir. No prob. I'll have that back to you before the day is over.

I inquire for fine details regarding the concept so that I may write an accurate piece, hung up the phone, scroll through my contacts and press "Sean Ace".

Sean Ace: What up?
Me: Bro, I just got a dope opportunity to potentially do spoken word on Big Boi's album.
Sean Ace: Fam…that's dope!
Me: I'm hella geeked, dude. Can I come thru and lay it at your spot?
Sean Ace: Hell yeah.
Voice in my head: The homie Ace…always coming through.
Me: Alright, thanks. I'll let you know when I'm on the way.
Sean: Bet.
Me: Alright then, peace.

I open the *Notes* app and begin drafting bars…

I zone out
on a search for the truth
looking for integrity

in this world and it's telling me
that real few and far between and it's scaring me
at the same time preparing me
so I turned open and wrote in a notepad
some dope, authentic lyrics,
now post that!
and it's gonna cost ya'
'cause lies are selling nowadays
and if you don't give into the machine
they'll say that you lost it

media outlets
leave me the hell alone
playing an age old game of telephone
intercepting and releasing a piece of truth
even with sarcasm
blasting so every Tom, Dick, Harry and Jamar has 'em
and they're leaking it out
deceiving the people about
a life they don't live or need to even be speaking about
emailing, blogging or posting or tweeting it out
making it seem
like I keep dirt under my rug, instead of sweeping it out

they be thinking it's sweet, but I doubt
that they want me to bring the street to their house
'cause then they want peace treaties
and my fam tells me to leave 'em
alone and get back on your grind and keep eating
'cause we're listening, so keep spitting it dope at 'em
that realness.
'cause those people that mind, they don't matter

malignant frien-emies
who knew fame came with a tumor
in disguise?
vicious lies and dangerous rumors.

I recite this about three or four times to begin to commit it to memory, record it in a voice memo, email it to myself, download it, convert it to an mp3 in iTunes, and then burn it to a CD and play it on repeat as I head from Maywood to Sean's crib on the Southside. It's about a 20-25 minute drive. By the time I arrive, I have the piece memorized. He gets into audio engineer mode and prepares my vocal levels. I record the poem and ask him to add record popping to the background to give it an old school vinyl feel. Around 7:22pm, I sent two audio files to Lo and send him a text as well letting him know that two mp3s of pure Columbian, uncut raw had been delivered to both his Comcast and Gmail. He calls me about 30 minutes later as I was getting ready to leave Sean's crib.

Lo: B!
Me: What's good, Boss?
Lo: Damn that was fast! I got someone that wants to talk to you.
Voice in my head: I bet money it's *Francis The Savannah Chittlin Pimp*.
Me: Okay.
Voice on the phone: Hello?
Me: What's up?
Voice on the phone: Yeah yeah, boy this is jammin. Dope. I just need you to cut it down to right at one minute. We're putting together the album and we wanna keep intros and interludes short.
Voice in my head: Oh snap, I think it's Big Boi!
Me: So, do you want me to spit it faster to fit one minute?
Voice on the phone: Naw, I like that pace, just do what you gotta do, I just need it to be one minute.
Me: Alright, cool. I can do that.
Lo: B! This is dope as hell! Big loves it, okay? So, just shorten it to about one minute and send it back.
Me: No problem, I got you.
Lo: Alright then. Bye.

Sean gives me a brief, paralyzed, blank stare of disbelief similar to the one that Martin, Pam, Gina and Cole gave him after saying he's headed to work. He daps me up, commends me on my progress and networking skillset, and then proceeds to set up another Pro Tools session.

Fast-forward to March of 2013. Big Boi's album is out and he's on the "*Shoes for Running World Tour*" with Killer Mike. Lo calls me and informs me that they're stopping in Chicago on May 1st to a venue called *Park West*. He wants to give me the opportunity to open the show with a ten minute performance slot. I graciously accept and begin planning my set.

I'm thinking about what two songs I should perform and what I should wear. I contact the good brother, legendary filmmaker and editor, E. Seals and put him on notice that I'd like to hire him to cover my sound check and performance for the tour stop. I start sharing the opportunity with my friends and extended family as I notice my name added to the bill on the ticket website. I tell my friend Rece, a choreographer from St. Louis and she offered to drive up to Chicago to dance for the performance and would tell one of her friends Regina as well. I contacted another friend, Chanel and asked her to come up with a dance for the performance. I call Isaac to be the drummer, George to play keys over the track, Duggy to DJ and Sondra to sing vocals. The day of the show, E. Seals brings along the good sister, and legendary filmmaker, Sanicole as a part of the crew for a 2nd camera angle. It's lit. I sent for the brother James Caldwell-Acha-Ngwodo, to style me and the fellas for the performance. Sondra helped with picking accessories, dresses and shoes for the ladies to wear and I hire Valencia to do their makeup.

We're all fresh, dressed like a million bucks. Imagine the movie *Harlem Nights*. I'm in a white tuxedo with black and white wingtips, the fellas are in black pants with white shirts and red ties, the ladies are in black and red dresses with black and white shoes, and Sondra is rocking a red dress with black and white heels. We all are pretty much aesthetically lit. Just before show time, Angelo says they'll delay the opening by five minutes and says that I could use that time for further prep or extend my set to 15 minutes. I decided to keep the set exactly how we rehearsed. A quality ten minute show would surely look better than an amazing two thirds of a 15 minute performance. There was no host, so I grab a wireless mic, get the crowd hype and then introduce myself from backstage.

After a dynamite opening performance, Lo comes out and demands that the crowd give us another round of applause and that they show support. We all take a bow. I immediately grab my merchandise bag and go into the crowd selling CDs and giving away glow-in-the-dark buttons during the DJ break before the next act. I studied Killer Mike and Big Boi's solo sets and watched the skillful turntablist expertise displayed by DJ Trackstar and Cutmaster Swiff. Killer Mike even hopped off stage at one point and was rapping in the crowd a'capella.

The next morning, Lo told me that their next show was in Milwaukee. I told him that was just under a two hour drive from Chicago. He said if we made it there, he would make sure that we could open at that show as well. I made the necessary phone calls and paid for gas to travel. The next night, we arrive in Milwaukee at *The Rave Eagle* minutes before load-in. I run into OutKast's drummer, Omar Phillips.

Omar: (*daps me*) what's up man, y'all opening here again?
Me: Yeah
Omar: We were just talking about y'all on the tour bus! Great show.
Voice in my head: Wow. OutKast's drummer thinks we're dope.

We smash the Milwaukee show. Afterwards, Lo pulls me aside and asks me how much did I spend on putting together the team for the Chicago show and how much was gas to get here and home. I told him around how much it cost. He pulls out a wad and counts a few bills off.

Lo: Here's some gas money. (*peels back more dollars*) Here's for what it cost you to put together the show. (*counts a few more bills*) Here's per Diem for your team, make sure they eat tonight.
Me: Thank you big bro.
Lo: Ain't no thang. I'll call you tomorrow afternoon after I speak to Big's manager. I'm going to try and get you to open the Atlanta show.
Voice in my head: Lo is the homie, for real.

Lo calls me the next day and tells me that I've been approved to open for Big in Atlanta at *The Masquerade*. He informs me that if I find a way to get to Atlanta, he'll take care of my team's lodging. I immediately put together a fundraiser via Eventbrite and share it on my Facebook to raise money for a 15-pasenger van, gas money and food for our trip to Atlanta and back. I raise the money in six days.

Plot twist! Big Boi ends up injuring his leg on tour. They push the Atlanta show from the first week of June to a September date. I recall that I have some September dates booked. Rewind back to March of that same year, my brother T. Murph and I attended the APCA (*The Association for the Promotion of Campus Activities*) national conference in Atlanta, GA. I booked about 12 schools; the majority of which were within a 100 mile radius of Atlanta. Back to real time, I check the email from Angelo saying that the new date for Big Boi in Atlanta is September 20th. I then check my emails from APCA and the very last date that I booked was for a college near Atlanta on

September 17th. That my friend is what you call GOD. "Divine synchronicity, we call that perfect timing…" (to quote the legendary, Jamaican wordsmith, Karega Bailey). I am so full at this moment. Everything has come together perfectly. This also means that I'll have one day to fly home, rent the van and drive the team down to Atlanta, and I'll have additional income to cushion the road trip and pay for my team to eat well.

The morning of the road trip, at the very last minute, the rental company I planned on using decides to tell me that they cannot accommodate me. I'm no quitter. After several attempts to everything in my personal power, I call up Granddad while en-route to his office. I slide into his office like Max Julien in *The Mack* with a wad of cash in hand for the rental and explain the scenario in detail (*because Grandad got the juice, all different types and ain't nobody got time for rent-a-car companies trying to stifle his grandson's entrepreneurial dreams*). Granddad trails me over to the *better* rental company, we pay for full coverage and I throw myself, Isaac and Duggy on as additional drivers.

Additional plot twist! I'm calling and rounding up the team to meet in certain locations on the south side and suburbs of Chicago so I can pick them up and we get a head start on the road. I call George to see where he is and he reminds me, "I'm in Chattanooga playing a gig with Mathien." I tell him, "Cool, I'll call you when we leave Nashville I think it's about an hour and a half from Chatt." I call James and he's in Indianapolis, which is also on the way. I call Isaac and he couldn't get out of a gig in Carbondale and couldn't meet us at the original departure point for the drive. Carbondale is five to six hours south of Chicago near the southernmost tip of Illinois and I've taken a road trip to Nashville, TN before. When leaving Carbondale, you take Illinois Route-13 East to Interstate-57 South and this runs into Interstate-24 East.

We leave Chicago on I-94 East and switch over to I-65 South which will run into Indianapolis. I recall while visiting Milton in Nashville that eventually I-24 and I-65 intersect there. I call Isaac and ask him to try and get someone to drive him from Carbondale to Nashville and leave about three hours before 11pm Central Standard Time because that's when we would arrive there. I even opened my Maps app and Googled a gas station near the highway for James to meet us in Indianapolis and for Isaac to meet us in Nashville. We pick up James at a BP on I-65 in Indianapolis and coordinate a bathroom break simultaneously. When we reach the city limits of

Nashville, I copy and paste the address (*I really shouldn't be texting and driving*) of the gas station and text Isaac where to meet us then paste that address into the GPS. We pick up Isaac and I thank the brother that drove him the distance to meet us and hand him some gas money for his trip back to Carbondale. I'm dog tired, either Duggy or Isaac decide to drive. I remember trying to fight sleep as we drove through the winding hills of Tennessee. I hate this stretch of zig-zag interstate with a passion; and it's raining! We reach a steep incline and I see the signs that read "Runaway Truck Ramp" so I know Chattanooga is near. We pick up George at this hotel and I jump back behind the wheel and we hit the road to Atlanta.

We arrive in Atlanta and Lo texts me the address to this beautiful, fully furnished home that he's rented for us near Turner Field. We load in and I try to get a few hours of sleep. The team disperses and picks rooms and starts prepping for tonight's show. Sound check took forever and kind of threw a monkey wrench in the schedule. Nonetheless, we hit the stage and showed out! We sell merch, enjoy the remainder of the show, and then load out. I recall meeting Sleepy Brown backstage and thinking he could be someone's bodyguard. I also saw Backbone and upon greeting him, he gave me some dope words of encouragement. The team and I grab something to eat and head back to the house.

I catch an flight early back to Chicago to host Ms. Vaughn and Meechy's Industry Standard fashion show while the team made sure that the house wasn't in shambles and that everyone got home safely. I checked in with Duggy every hour or so. By the fourth check-in he told me that he was running low on the travel money that I gave him. I immediately send a *Quick Pay* for more money between hosting. They arrive safely and on the morning of the show, I meet Isaac at his house to pick up the van and return it. Mission accomplished.

Later that day, Angelo informed me that Big had seven more dates left on his tour and if I could meet him at the locations that I can open. The next location after Atlanta was Chattanooga. A few days later, I catch a flight to Nashville and my home girl Sabrina Walker picks me up from the airport and drops me at the Greyhound station and I catch the bus to Chattanooga. I arrive and catch a local taxi to the venue called *Track 29*. I told the driver that I was a rapper and he replies, "You ever heard of Big K.R.I.T.? My grandson DJs for him, DJ Wally Sparks." We have a conversation about music and I then tweet DJ Wally Sparks and let him know that his uncle is cool.

He drops me at *Track 29* and I see Big's crew and Sleepy.

They're all like, "Hey, what's up Real T@lk?" and greeting me like I'm one of the fam. The whole crew made me feel like I belonged. I recall them inviting me to grab some food as soon as it came. There was no "sonning" of any sort. All respect. I'll never forget that. We rocked Chattanooga on Tuesday and Asheville, NC on Wednesday. Angelo told me that the next two shows in Wilmington, NC and Philly were festivals so I wouldn't be able to open. I told him that I'll find some business and meet them at the stop in Boston at the Paradise Rock Club on Sunday.

Early Thursday morning, I look up a map of North Carolina and see where Ashville is in proximity to Charlotte because I am more than certain that a greyhound operates between those cities. I go on greyhound and purchase a one way ticket to Charlotte. When I board the bus, I log on to the WiFi post on all of my social medias the following message: "To my poetry peoples, are there any sets in Charlotte?" I receive several replies on my status and in my inbox as well as a few text messages that point to a brother named Jaycee that hosts a weekly Thursday night in Charlotte that's been running for years. I look him up on Facebook and inbox him a well thought out non-prima Donna message letting him know that I'm on tour passing through Charlotte and I would be through to support his show. I said nothing like, "Can you give me a feature?" or accolade-filled paragraph messages demanding a spot on the list.

Side note: when heading to a set that I've never been to before, I tread very respectfully with the host; I greet the hometown poets and the people with the love and manners that my OGs from the Chicago poetry scene taught me by example. On the contrary when I am called to the mic to share, I proceed to blaze in a disrespectfully dope manner of overkill. I acquire his number from another fellow poet and give him a call. He welcomes me with open arms and says that he'll let me spit at least two pieces that night. I arrive in Charlotte and call my home girl, Davida whom becomes my impromptu tour guide for Charlotte. I do my thing on stage, network, and sell merch.

Friday morning, I catch a Megabus to Washington D.C. and connect with one of my younger frat brothers, Louis who was enrolled in Law School at Howard University (*by the time this book is published, he will have his law degree*). He picks me up in a white Jaguar and I congratulate him on doing dope things and progressing as a melanated brother in America. On the way to his crib, we catch up and he tells me that he's swamped with briefs and schoolwork. He hands me the keys to his car and says, "Here you go, you good,

Hollywood. Go wherever you need to go; just put gas in the whip." I get word that "Love the poet" is hosting "*Be Free Fridays*" in Baltimore at the *Eubie Blake Center* on Howard and the good brother "Droopy, the Broke Baller" (that hosts "*Spit Dat")* is the feature. I put some gas in the tank and drive up to Baltimore. I greet the poets and people in the building. I get to rock a poem and watch Droopy blaze his feature and take notes because he's been doing this longer than I; plus he's a comedian, actor and an overall dope writer. After the show, I sell a few CDs and then pack up. I offer him a ride back to his home in D.C. We chop it up and trade a few stories about touring and the poetry scene. He drops a few precious gems of history and performance on me that I'm forever grateful for.

Saturday morning, I'm not sure where I'm headed next or when, but I eventually have to be in Boston by Sunday night. I get an inbox from a soror of mine that I met in Phoenix by that name of Tursha who was in D.C. with her cousin who's an attorney, and they were headed to the *Busboys* in Hyattsville to eat which is coincidentally minutes from Louis's spot. I tell him to meet me at Busboys so I can introduce him to Tursha and network with her cousin because I'm sure could maybe give him a few pointers regarding law school. We arrive and there are no seats. We see a group of elders and they invite me and Louis to sit with them while we're waiting for a table. Three minutes into conversation, we find out that we're sitting across from a few photographers, a filmmaker and a BET executive. I tell them that I'll be back on Wednesday to open for Big Boi and Killer Mike at The Howard Theater which is the final tour date. We exchange contact information, and I invite them out to the show.

While checking Facebook, I get a message from my big homie Dave Maxime, SIUC alumni, a Chicago native, filmmaker and hip-hop enthusiast. I told him that Big's tour stopped in Brooklyn on Tuesday. He said he'll be in Bed Stuy all weekend and next week. I asked if I could crash with him tonight and he said it was cool. I immediately search the *Bolt Bus* schedule and see that there's one leaving D.C. soon headed to New York City. I give my farewells to the elders, Tursha and cousin Angelique. Louis drops me at the *Bolt Bus* stop and I make it in the nick of time.

I arrive in NYC and Dave texts me specific details as to which trains to catch to Brooklyn. I come out of the station and meet him with his dog, "Phife" (*sadly, both his pet and the beloved MC he was named after passed around the same time*). I ask him about any public transportation between here and Boston and he suggests that we rent a car because he can get a discount. "Just *Quick Pay* half of the final amount, cover the gas and drive half of the trip." I accept the offer and Sunday afternoon, we set out to Boston. We arrive in time for sound check. *Momskillet* just happened to be in Boston for work. I arrange for her to meet Angelo, and he seated her in the VIP booth. I rock Boston and sell some merch. We hit the road and get back to Brooklyn around three ante meridian.

With Monday being a day to kill, I used this time to duplicate more CDs and find out about any open mics to spit at. I find out that it is *"Open Mic Monday"* at *The Nuyorican Poets Café* in Manhattan. The doors open at 8pm, but the line starts forming around 6 or 7pm and stretches around the block. We arrive about 6:30pm and the line is about 40 people deep. I find the list and it's completely full. I will not be defeated. I leverage a comp ticket to my show tomorrow at Brooklyn Bowl and finesse my way on the open mic list to spit sixth. I spit fire and then stay to enjoy the rest of the show. I do not perform and leave immediately (*and give a big middle finger to the culture art form and audience because my OGs from the Chicago poetry scene have taught me respect and open mic etiquette*). After the show, I run into the good brother *Mick Jenkins* in a cypher outside the venue. I commend him on his art and dap him and his crew up. Dave and I head back to his spot in Bed Stuy making one stop by the bodega on Marcus Garvey Blvd to grab a bite to eat and a ginger beer. I adore ginger beer, especially *Reed's*.

Tuesday afternoon I go to get a haircut at a barber shop that Dave recommended. I walk in and see my girlfriend, Whitney sitting in the waiting area with a Cheshire cat grin. I give her a big hug and kiss and give her the "How Sway?" face. This woman flew into New York City for one day to support her man. That was dope. I also think to myself that I'm glad I wasn't being loose and unfaithful on the road because this pop up visit could be a disaster! I text a few friends and extended family in NYC and invite them to the show. I get a call from the legendary, award-winning poet, author and big brother of the Chicago poetry scene, J. Ivy. He says he and his better half (Tarrey) are in Harlem and would try to come through the show. I get their information, and add it to the comp list. The brother from *Nuyorican* that I added to the comp list is at the door and calls me because the venue is 21+ and he's underage. I tell him that it's not going to happen, but I get his mailing address in New Jersey, I purchase a Big Boi album and have him autograph it and the next morning mail it off as a consolation gift. He texted me about a week later and thanked me for the personalized CD. I get on stage, do my thing and sit down to enjoy the remainder of the show. During Big Boi's set, he performs *Kryptonite* and me and the other openers got to come on stage and get the crowd hype with him. Dave caught a dope candid of Big Boi, Killer Mike, Sleepy Brown and I on stage doing a two-step during the hook. It's posted on my Instagram and Facebook somewhere.

The next morning, I wake up early and drive Whitney to JFK to fly home. A few hours later, Dave drives me to Manhattan to catch the *Bolt Bus* to D.C. During the ride, I call Kamikazi (one of the filmmakers that I met at *Busboys*) and tell her the time of my sound check so she can meet me at The Howard Theatre. I call the good brother Josh (*a director and filmmaker I met about a year ago in Manasssas, VA at Spirits-N-Lyrics*) and tell him about the opportunity that I have and he agrees to meet me at sound check as well. A couple years ago, I met a brother who went by the name of *DJ ChubbESwagg* who is originally from California and holding everything down on Howard University's campus party-wise. I contact him via Twitter and he texts me and says that he's in D.C. I ask him how much to DJ during my opening set. He says that he's been booked to spin for the entire show between acts and would DJ and help me hype the crowd during my set for no charge. Before the doors open, I step outside and Kami and Josh capture interview footage for my documentary series, *Memoirs of A Modern-Day Griot, Episode Four.* I greet every one of the servers, waitresses, and bar tenders and give them a glow-in-the-dark Real T@lk logo button. One or two of them bought a CD before the show started. I run into a brother by the name of Demont Pinder who's in the backstage stairway painting a portrait of Big Boi on the wall.

After the show, I hop into the crowd and greet the fans, sell CDs and give out buttons. During load-out, I say peace to all of the engineers, film crews, photographers, and DJs. I ask Killer Mike and Sleepy Brown for their emails and they both insist that I take their phone numbers. My brother Karega came through and offered to give me a ride back to Louis's spot. Before I leave, I'm looking for Big Boi and Angelo to thank them for the opportunities. I run into Angelo at the door of Big's tour bus. I thank him for everything and he tells me that Big is onboard finishing his last meet-and-greet. I told him I'll just step on and wave bye so I don't interrupt. He insists and brings me on the tour bus.

Lo: Naw, it's cool, just come on in.

Me: Alright.

Voice in my head: He's busy. Just say bye and shake his hand.

Me: (*waves hand*) Alright then Big, I'm out bro!

Big Boi: (*to fan*) 'preciate it. (*to me*) Aye, hold up, come here!

Me: What's up?

Big Boi: Man…the video…where you rappin…, with the fruit?…Boi Stop! You be snappin'. I'm talking like… lyrically, better than a lot of dudes out now.

Me: (*daps him up*) Thank you, Fam. I just want to thank you for the opportunity to rock with you on these tour dates.

Big Boi: You're welcome, you're welcome, man.

Voice in my head: I know what you're thinking…don't do it Brandon.

Me: Yo, I wrote a hook that I think you'd like and I could hear you and Dre on it, or you and Killer or even you and me. It's called "LXG" check it out:

introducing
two of the illest, realest spittin' it
south of the Mason-Dixon line
and eastward of the Mississip'
yes, yes, y'all
all of you should come and get with this
literary league of extraordinary gentlemen!

two of the illest, realest spittin' it
south of the Mason-Dixon line
and eastward of the Mississip'
yes, yes, y'all
all of you should come and get with this
literary league of extraordinary gentlemen!

Big Boi: Aww yeah yeah yeah, that's jamming!

Me: Thanks. I could hear that over like an 88 or 90bpm tempo beat by Organized Noize.

Big Boi: (*smiles*) Okay, so when are you coming to the A to record?

Voice in my head: Little does he know that you have a half segment left on a buddy pass and my bags are already packed.

Me: (*looks at army duffel and backpack*) I got my bags now, what up?

Big Boi: You can ride on the bus with us.

Lo: (*interrupts*) Big, there's no room. (*to me*) B, I'm not trying to block or anything, there's just not enough space.

Big Boi: Lo, we can make room, and we can put someone from here on the promo van. (*to me*) Excuse us for a minute.

Me: No problem.

(*I exit the bus. About 60 seconds later, Lo invites me back on the bus.*)

Big Boi: (*sighs and smiles*) Alright, we don't have enough space on here, but I'll be back in the A tomorrow. Imma take about a day to relax and then I'll be in the studio all day Friday and Saturday, 'cause I got a bunch of beats in my inbox and they're all jamming. Lo gon' give you my information.

Me: (*daps him up*) Okay bet. Thanks. I'll be in touch.

I step off the bus and give Angelo a hug. I thank him again and he hinted at a record deal being not far in my future career. I reply, "That's what's up, but before any of that, I'm interested in a management representation with *The Redding Group*". He smiles, "I'm sure we can arrange that, B. I'll email you." October of 2013, I sign a management deal with Angelo Redding and *The Redding Group.*, December of 2013 I make a trip to Atlanta, meet DJ Toomp, Ray Murray, DJ Cutmaster Swiff, Rick Walker and a few other record producers.

I proceed to record the first of many sessions at *Stankonia*.

confidence

I got a fascination
with imagination
I got *passion* naked
and left the quo-status waiting
got my dreams pregnant,
pulled out fast
broke up with the standard
and became an outcast
and after being casted out
people got bored with regular stuff
and so I'm crackin' now!
an intelligent gangster
with a life expectancy
of 21, gliding, with a pig flying next to me
a while ago they didn't want to mess with me
now they want a side of Alexander with an extra B
wait 'til they hear my acceptance speech
like: "Lord, thank you for all of these blessings G,
thank the trendy for what not to do
I thank the community
thank the haters for obstacles that turned into opportunities
I'm thankful for everything
that I ought to get,
but didn't receive because of politics.

if money was time

if money was time
I wouldn't be tardy with mine
head back to the future
with *Doc* & *Marty McFly*

being ahead or on time
has mad advantages
you can watch at your watch
but you can't really tamper with
the clock never stops
that's really why you can't handle it
you can only specialize in time-waste-management

some are living without a tock
don't take it for granted like a countertop
when I was out I saw
a bunch of people crowd a mall
let me tell about it y'all
they was shouting all loud and all
waiting in a line
just to sit inside
spending time
hours & minutes to get in *Finishline*

came early to be late
drove out wasting petrol
in sleeping bags and seats
people kept gettin stepped on
this man said he ain't a *klepto*
and he had to be fresh, so
he spent last two weeks saving seconds to get the retros!

I told him people shoot for those
he says he'll sock anyone in his path
'cause it ain't cool to go around being defeated

"I'll run outta time before I lose my sole."
repeat…
I'm like whoa,
it ain't a game, better change that
the other day *Flavor Flav* got his chain snatched
on the meanest block flossing his bling and watch
some *Minute-men* stuck him up and cleaned his clock
and made his breathing stop
slowed down his tempo
BPM, beats per minute, yeah that's the info
on him so
cherish your time and make sure that you live bro
and watch the people that keep their brims low
they keeping 'em blocked
'cause real lies are realized by real eyes
and they be blinking a lot
they might be the reaper ready to reach for the Glock

meanwhile "dime-pieces"
chase brothers with timepieces
fronting like
they're some balling-ass time keepers
but I won't front like I don't grind
Black Panther fist-Rolex
I call it *right on*-time
analog, digital
and it's all critical
listen to
lyrical witticisms
while I spit a few

my heartbeat's keeping the pace and
while I'm breathing and shaking
people are hating on my synchronization
the boom, bap, bap
drumbeating and bass-ing
that resembles a step team stampeding the pavement

people are paying, but I'm keeping respect
turning down Nike endorsements
like, "no you can't keep me in check

I'm not a routing number
not a food stamp voucher-hunter
no place for games
less recreation
so reckless creation
leaves no order, Money
or money order
they don't accept no check

you'd best protect your neck
because in retrospect hindsight is 20/20
and I just seen a *sankofa* bird on a treadmill

running out of time, legs real
big like he's been kicking infinity times
no historic identity, life
twisted in the head still

grandfather clock
told *father time* to come, now.
and wash his heir to the throne
so he have his son *Dial*

real sharp off of the head
Kung Lao

mr. write

she calls me Mr. Right
she tells me to grip her tight
she says, "I'll never run out on you. If I do, I'll just die.
see Boo, I love our relationship and love life,
'cause it's never give-and-take with you
it's just right!"

when I first met shorty, she was working for the bank
it's like that gig had her enslaved
hooked up to a chain
at the counter
and before the counter would give the clerk
the number on the display
onto the paper she would write customers' names
and it made her
job really that simple and plain
but I chose to take her
and separate her from those chains
so I could make her
useful for writing
more than a digit or phrase
on just some paper
and sitting there wasting away
so I said, "baby, I'mma take you back to see my pad,
and if it gets late, I got a cover and sheets, you can lay sleep on that.
and that old job, you'll never work another week, in fact,
when you're rolling with me, you'll never have to complete a task!"

she calls me Mr. Write
she tells me to grip her tight

she says, "I'll never run out on you, if I do I'll just die.
see boo, I love our relationship and love life,
'cause it's never give-and-take with you it's just right!"
my last girlfriend
was a yellow redbone
she was way too sharp and always led head-strong
I should've known straight from the gate
she had low self-esteem,
she was always erasing mistakes
it really wasn't working for me
she eventually got dull
trying to be too perfect for me
you can tell her that you heard it from me
'cause I'd much rather scribble out the page
so I can remember what I say
I see mistakes as perfect imperfections
but see perfection
she was too overly obsessed with
I said, "Baby, you're a basic kinda crazy,
you got me embarrassed to claim you as my lady,
plus when it comes to the paper that I make
and give it to you at a certain angle you're kinda shady.
now you're lazy, you just sit there stationary,
in addition to wasting my paper misusing my stationery."
I see this as a learned lesson and I'll take it,
because I could've been investing in replacements.
but it got down to the point
where she was like a professional eraser
so I'm confessing that I just had to erase her.

the tell-lie-vision

radio with a face
moving pictures
in a box
with audio on the scene
and all of you are going to pay
to satisfy all of your craves
in addition to (little by little) depleting all of your dreams
my Technicolor display
as exciting as it may seem
has been used for entertainment
messages in between
the lines and all of the space
stretching across my screen
since circa nineteen
hundred and twenty-six
commercialized in black and white
and then coloring after this
put in an insulated cord
or a satellite turning dish
and I'll become interchangeable
turning into what you wish

but see this is what you miss,
once you envision me (literally)
I enter into
your mental memory disk
and you begin to mimic me
again, again
and your kids
grow up in front of me,
run to me,

and come to me over you

and it is an ugly truth
'cause it's monkey see, monkey do
so while you're working
making your green
they don't distinguish between
fake and what's on the tube

and you can only blame it on you
although, somehow it is semi-entertaining to you,
once they interpret the behavior
begin misbehaving on you
because principal expelled them
so they start rebelling on you
and I start telling the news
don't get mad
and try getting rid of and selling me, dude
I wasn't the one
that packaged me up
and tried to sell me to you!
So you might as well get used
to me chilling in the middle and center
of living rooms
and get used to
sitting and watching me as a fiend
cause I just came thru
new and improved
with a plasma screen
I am the trash machine
or the idiot box
that you sit up and watch,
listen,
turn it on
and off
when static comes

you hit it on the top
like shook up grape soda
that you got and you know it's gonna "POP"
I am the gift
that you would tell
Santa to get for Christmas
along with a strong
antenna to get the picture
like a camera's mission
managing to turn
whoever's behind the lens
into mannequins with the pixels
and it's damaging to your mental
you can't stand
but to tune in frantic
and that is the issue
it is official
that I can no longer count the haters
I've turned you grouchy neighbors
into couch potatoes
you can't even doubt the ratings

in the beginning
my image diminished you
from the minute you
witnessed to
these thirty second
and minute-long intervals
within the shows projected
meaning you were already finished dude!
because of you I'm getting views
and all you can do
is bring and make me more
all those commercials you hate
are purposely placed
just so you can appreciate me more

so if you don't see what you like
and want what you hear off
I suggest you go blind,
close your eyes,
or slice your ears off!
and just think...
If all what America watches
reflects what they do
and their actions
then I definitely could be used
as an interaction
to spark, motivate,
move and influence the masses.
not saying that this is what happened
just calling a spade a spade
and saying Uncle Sam's possible actions
simply stating the facts and
only a fraction
of those that hear this feel me
of the fellas livin'
so I'll break it down...
I'm the one,
the only,
the television.

thoughts of a drunken scholar

I stagger down college streets
up Illinois Route 51
and college street
I'm actually a scholar, see
but, I'm tired of being looked up to!
I wanna do what I want to!
so what if I have a few too many drinks every now and then
so what if I spend the majority
of these 16 weeks downing gin
shots,
doused with sin
while hanging out with friends not
knowing,
well not knowing
but realizing
that this I'm still fighting
mature childhood nightmare
that's been there
since big wheel cycling

so I turn to this bottle
for two reasons:
first, because by the time
I'm 100 proof full
it looks just big enough
for me to hide in,
and shoot,
if I put a Corona lid on it
and turn it tight man,
can't nobody make they way right in!
the other reason that I
confide in

this container that I reside in
is 'cause, although I don't seem like a punk,
I got low self-esteem as a drunk
so I fit right in.
I swallow its contents
so I can feel full
and poke fun at it
'cause it's empty inside
just like I was.
This nonsense doesn't comprehend now since
I'm tipsy
cause I overstand statements
and I don't even get me.
in the end,
when I'm done laughing
at this liquor jug
that I weekend-ly
pause my life with,
I'll just vomit all this gin
and end up feelin' just like it ...
empty
so I might as well take another sip "G".

financial aid office

Jam:
But, I swear
I'm in no position
to pay this tuition!
How come the president
and his administration
can't pay for this statement?
I'm a first generation
student coming from a single mother kid.
Why can't the government
just change the page
and put me under it?

Here we go again…
All I am is an undergrad,
not pissed, but a little under mad
and upset
because this underclassman was misinformed
that if I came to college
I could immediately get my mission going
so I get to class,
and the professor says "You're an imposter!"
He says, "in this 3-hour credited class
you're not on the registered roster!"
He said that "it's gonna cost ya'
so go to the website of FAFSA
and get Pell and Map granted
so you can finally prosper!"

So I'm thinking I'm all good
cause these grants take about seven days to take effect
but the college takes like two more weeks
to collect and accept the check!

So you're wondering,

"Can they lose the amount?"
and that's what you're asking
because the status of your student account
won't let you sign up for classes
so I'm phone taggin' and surfin'
back and forth to financial aid
arguing with student workers
and one of them finally said
"Either make this bill pay happen at once,
or sit at home waiting
for it to pay in
by the better half of the month!"

Fred:
But,
I swear I'm in no position
to pay this tuition!
How come the president
and his administration can't pay for this statement?
My folks wealthy and separated
their relationship is hectic
so the family contribution expected
is much lower
than the actual amount projected

now, why did I get so little for financial aid?
I was counting on federal and state
to have my finances paid
so I get this letter from Uncle Sam
and then and I opened it
to see what it said
and under the letter head
The first line read:

Jam: Greetings family of Fred,
but we regret
to inform you
that it's not our fault your daddy said
he would contribute no more bread
from outta his wallet now
that you break-ing
past the age of eight-teen
and college bound
and mama can contribute
only so much
from outta her bank account
and bag of Prada now
so your pride
you better go swallow now
and get you a job at McDonald's pal
to pay all those bills
with more dollars and cents-es
on this long list of university expenses!
(Fred: In a nut shell...)
your folks make too much dough,
provolone and gouda
for you to request
a government over loan for moulah!

Fred:
So what do I do, y'all?
Both parents are on my financial aid application
however, one of them
actually supports me on paper and off
but the school don't know that
so all I'm thinking now is...
Man, I wish colleges would promote this kind of stuff
as much as they do their brand new buildings!

the LINK card

the saying goes:
if you give a man a fish,
he'll eat for a day,
if you teach him how to fish,
he eats for a lifetime!

government gives you LINK
to cut monthly cost out of your budget
not for you to be dependent of it

that's teaching a man
to teach a man
how to give away fish
so the only one that knows how to fish
is in control of all of them
most black folks see this as a "hook-up"
and young ones look up to them like:
"ahhh, this is the good stuff!"
but it ain't much
it's simply a small part of the hooves from
this mule that they present in
blinding us
halfway
with 40/40 Acre-Vision

observationist misses the point

keep using the phrase
"he or she should know better"
you'll really show them.

self-broken heart

I used to have this girl
I wanted to give the world
But I was paranoid
Because I stole her from this boy
We tried to make it work
for whatever that it was worth
it wasn't right from the start
I ended up breaking my own heart

well it was something like that, but it was different
my sister told me to sit up and listen, but I didn't
my brother told me to live for the moment and be pimping
give them the cold shoulder after stroking in the kitten
a little manipulation
then they're open for submission
after the penetration
she will be forever vacant
(and so will you)
but then she will begin the chasing
wherever you move
she will be forever adjacent
blocking them other women
from being up in your face and
telling them dudes to keep it moving
she wasn't playing
"you can do what you wanna
with no if, ands, or no maybes
everything will be cool" she said,
"it will be all gravy
I will play my role
as long as you don't try and play me
not sure if it shows
but boo, I do love you greatly

so, if you go or do me wrong
my heart will be aching
so don't try to sleep on me
'cause I am not lazy
but see I have been known
to be a bit crazy
if you do it first
I'll be a different person
you'll be facing
nothing equals the hurt
so I'll take your shirts
and then I'll place 'em
first in bleach detergent
and then go burn them up in the basement!"

I said: "you'll do what?
you'll take my shirts and then you'll place 'em,
first, in bleach detergent
and then go burn them up in the basement?"
she said: "I will only go further,
that is, if you make me,
so please don't make me, (make me)
'cause you are my baby, Baby."

so now the story ends
and another one begins
of a self-broken heart
that I could've prevented from the start
but now I gotta mend
I thought that I was on
damn…
where the hell did I go wrong?
until I figure it
I'll be rapping this song:
I guess you'll never know what you got 'til it's gone
~~I used to have this girl~~

~~I wanted to give the world~~
~~but I was paranoid~~
I guess you'll never know what you got 'til it's gone
~~I used to have this girl~~
~~I wanted to give the world~~
~~but I was paranoid~~
I guess you'll never know what you got 'til it's gone

well, maybe that's true,
if she would've stuck around
would I be the same dude?
would I be mature or would I be rude?
the latter of the 2
well, that is what I choose
'cause I see it was She
that I had to lose
I may have lost forever,
but I pray it ain't the truth,
if it's not the truth,
then it'll be a blessing,
but if it is the truth
then fellas listen, it's a lesson,
a lesson
a part of this confession
I'm going to explain
so let me take a breath in...

because she was no longer
tolerating my actions
and took her love away
from out the reach of my grasping
she allowed maturity
to happen faster
by administering some disciplinarian action
I was no longer able to act with malice ,
receive abundance of love to have and ration...

foreshadowed adult-ing

I want a tribe y'all
several babies,
six or seven, eight and
melanated
with knowledge of self celebrated
I look forward to
being a father
to sons being a barber
and when I see that their mama
is too tired to do hair
I'll be seating my daughters
proceeding to part a
section of two-strand twists
with a little grease at the start of
where I do move hands, wrists
keeping my arm up
and this
man can just
teach manners
please, ma'am, sir
preach can, leave can't first
don't go by self
excelling to get to the spot
parked closest to the door
tell 'em together we'll get the lot
yes sir, even more
and most importantly
there's a time to
shed and get over tears
they'll get in a little trouble
and let it be over peers
but no felonies over here
disciplinarian style?
instilling integrity over fear.

perception is reality

ugly people look sexy to *drunk* people,
just like smart people look crazy to *dumb* people.

they thought the Wright brothers were high as hell

off that fluid,
'til they flew it,

now, they're fly as hell.

epistemophobia

reporting live from the NASDAQ
ignorance is booming
more than a little bit
and information's losing
less exercise of brain memory
'cause smartphones got everybody stupid

news keeps you sitting still
scared to love or let GOD take the steering wheel
scared of what you reflect in the mirror still
that's fear...
false evidence appearing real

still...
first 48 got us desensitized
to the value of life
and black genocide
reality television lied
misrepresenting wives
depicting bitter, black women
bickering sipping wine

less human interaction that requires conversation,
there's an app for that
so we're afraid to love, parents scared of kids
so petrified of failure that we're afraid to live

support increases experience

when you have someone
there to catch you when you fall,
you take more chances.

showtime

one for the money,
yes sir, two for the show
a couple of years ago
circa 2004
when G and his plans got
moved away
and I started cruising that Amtrak
thru the state
me and my ship stayed up in Neely
and everyday we'd look up at the ceiling
headphones bumping that KanYeezy
College Dropout on repeat
had a breezy
and my notebook
and plus my refund
looking forward to U.A. open mics
'cause it would be one
taking placement
in the basement of the dining hall
I and all
of the lyricists spitting it kind of raw
just like some undercooked poultry
yeah we was rhyming, dog
scatting, beatboxing and rapping
in a café that was kind of small
it was exciting au-
tomatic rhyming
E.Dot Clipse in cyphers yelling
with Turtle, Rashod and Relic
back when he was kind of dreaded,
had them baby locs
they'd be rocking in the area
and it made me watch
'cause it was showtime!

Sometimes on purpose
I would be late
to stay in better shape,
17th and Roosevelt
I would race to catch the Pace
I find it ironic before I start
I'd make it all the way to Park Forest
starting from Forest Park
with notebooks and new rhymes
I'd hop on the blue line
take it down to Clark and Lake
then get off in due time
transfer to a loop line
and stand off
in it 'til I made a grand halt
at Wabash and Randolph
I ran off
of it with plenty of haste and
energy and bought a ticket at Millennium Station
A to, let's see, Route F selected
down south Chicago on the Metra Electric
better than the L
no blacks in action
no loose square sellers
or loud rats reacting
just leather seats for my back relaxing
'til Authentik picked a brother up
back in Matteson

reciting my best verse 'til my mouth hurts
from the west 'burbs to the south 'burbs
I'm doing this so when I spout words
my engineer Sean Ace
can produce a better sound worth

reciting my best verse 'til my mouth hurts
from the west 'burbs to the south 'burbs
I'm doing this so when I spout words
my engineer Sean Ace
can produce a better sound worth

one for the money,
yes sir, two for the show

common sensibility

if GOD gave us this Earth,
you'd think she'd expect us to
treat it right...or nah?

so intelligent freestyle

she said you're just so intelligent
speech so eloquent
approached this young fella with
an umbrella smelling like a heaven scent
I said this must be heaven sent
(*sniffs*)...this is heaven scent
from GOD
swear to Bob!
no embellishment
and I reckon if
she smells this good on the regular
then she probably tastes decadent
I could pleasure her measurements
but...that's irrelevant
loving her whole element
approached real delicate
displaying etiquette
making it evident
stating it plain
I'm trying to set precedents
not make it rain with dead presidents
she was kind of hesitant
then she replied: "that's excellent!
I got my own career,
place of residence,
I won't check your messages
won't marry you and then meddle with
your emotions to leave you and receive a settlement."
I said: that's cool, I love your rhetoric
besides, school and Sallie Mae left me in a deficit
so if you did, you wouldn't get a lump sum or plump estimate
although my education was accredited
but, let me get straight to the point
I think you're elegant

but pickup lines never win
so I want to be direct
instead of try angles
delta,
elephant,
in the room,
awkward,
not me!
it's never been
them other weak brothers you can jettison
toss them out
roll with this 6'2" specimen
with hella' melanin
to show you the limit ain't sky, It's indefinite
I got ambition
King don't pedal no street medicine
treat Queen with feet rub in tub
with sweet petals
on thee pedestal
she no come down
unless me tell her to:
"come here, me'll make ya scream
like tea kettles do!"
or tea kettles when
they're ready and...
hot to pop
nope, I'm not arrogant
I'm just relevant
those other merry men, they're an experiment
Chicago, pro mascot, b-ball, excrement
they need development

free for sale

whose idea was it
to bottle water and sell?
that's some GREEDY stuff.

not here for the sarcastic irony

Harriet Tubman
was not a capitalist.
So…yeah, no thank you.

jealousy

buddy with the locks
fifteen
west side of the Chi
Holy City he resides
and the sky
ain't the limit
just the block
where he's trying to survive
gang-banging wit his friends
'cause its "ride 'til we die"
he saw a lady that he used to see
a teacher at the school where he used to be
he remembers she use to keep
setting him these hoops to leap through

she's getting bread out the ATM
he remembers her playing him
like, "I'm finna get off work and go back to the 'burbs"
she could've been saving him
she gets in her Mercedes Benz
puts the seatbelt on her waist and then
there he was,
bandana on his neck
with a gun in her face
and she says, "don't take my ends!
here you go, take this here!
nevermind, please, just let me live!
I know you're fed up,
you just gotta keep your head up"
he's like, "shut up!
I'm sick of seeing this
church, liquor store,
liquor store, church, church
gimme yo' purse!

I'm "on dummy"
life ain't sunny
ain't nobody care about me since birth
so I'm just hurt, I got no money
now I'm on dirt with an empty stomach
in this economy it ain't no work
I go to apply
they be like, "no sir"
so we're gonna be moving D on the block
so the fiends and the peons
can chief on
and tweak on the rocks
and we're gonna stockpile
glock 9s
post at the stop signs
and we're gonna plot
so get out the car
gimme that
just get out the car
I would take the path y'all tell us
but I'm just jealous

verse two, meet Ashley
she's only 18
and you have to see
this pretty girl has to be
killing the freshman class
if you're asking me
and she goes fast
but gets no tickets
plus she's sluggin'
boy she's wicked
yeah she's thick and
built like a grown woman
from the steroids in all that chicken

six piece mild
don't even need liquor
she'll get wild
and you can get with her
she's one of them party girls
at the top of her grades
that'll play for any man that picks her
but by next year
she was tired of hit-and-run
her roommate Kate
getting gifts and love
from her boyfriend Chris on campus
so Ashley's like, "yeah, I'mma get me some"
'til one day Kate had an argument
with Chris and left the apartment
she went to Eastern for the weekend
to meet with some people to party with
she told Ashley
if Chris comes back to the crib
before I come back from the trip
don't let him back in the crib
but when he came back
she took him to the back
and then got it cracking with him

Chris goes with the flow
They're both thinking that nobody knows
but Kate left her I.D. on the bed
and heard them
so here she goes through the door
she's contemplating her options
she could sit, listen and watch them
or she could smack Chris from off top and
then pull Ashley out and start boxing

Chris says, "Ashley wait,

we gotta stop this.
Aye, what are you on, with me?"
she says, "My daddy wasn't there to teach me love
so I'm desperate and I'm lonely.
See, I imagined you coming on to me
and I got overzealous
and I see how you treat her
and I want that
so I'm just jealous"

roommate Kate
eyes full of tears
her heart forever stained black
she came thru when Ash went to sleep
moved out overnight
and never came back
time went on
Ashley was growing sick
big stomach
over six months
no period growing thick
she figured it gotta belong to Chris
she told him take ownership
they argue
but Chris goes along with it
the whole time not knowing if
the fetus growing belongs to him
Kate came to visit town
got wind of the news that went around
saw Chris at Chick-Fil-A
and said it may not be his
shorty used to get around

he get's a call
she in labor
he goes to the ER

signs them papers
they gave him a swab
time came later
they told him it ain't his baby
he said, "I'm gone."
she had nothing
but the baby boy
from out of her tummy
afraid to raise a child alone
she put him up for adoption
and named him Buddy...

Buddy with the locks
fifteen,
west side of the Chi
Holy City he resides
and the sky ain't the limit
just the block where he's trying to survive
gang-banging wit his friends
'cause it's "ride 'til we die" . . .

but, it's cleaner though!

bottled water says
"contains calcium chloride."
but...I'm not swimming.

give 0% shine to suckas

when you speak ill of
your ex, it makes *you* look wack.
go somewhere and heal.

the heist: stickin' up sallie mae

3 summers after graduation
Juneteenth 2012, no exaggeration
I got fed up after waiting
for a callback from 3 places where I put in applications
with resumes; no procrastinating
but see, I been unemployed so long
my own people think I'm black and lazy
a while ago they said congratulations
now I'm overqualified with no job
no wonder why I'm acting crazy
I keep getting calls from this aggressive-passive lady,
letters sayin: "you gotta pay me."
sorry, I don't have it baby
Sallie Mae be acting shady
her rep replied like: "what about next week?"
I told them to tell Sallie maybe
I hung up tried to put it all behind me
but no matter where I go
she would always find me
but today I had an epiphany
I said that I wouldn't let her get to me

I paid for school to get a job
just to get a job so I can pay for school
I'm getting grown
student loans
I think I let them take me for a fool

nope, instead I'mma get to her, though
I'mma rob her for all her dough
and give it out to the poor
broke, young scholars
living it thru the war

community college students
that plan on switching to a four-year
university with higher tuition
that probably won't take their credits
if they're under a hundred digits
I mean...level—
under one hundred level
I'll also give most of it back to
undergraduate rebels

and these grad students
going for their masters
working for "the Massa"
overworking their asses
researching daily
taking night classes
credit scores dying
lowering in caskets

them guys got patience
but he ain't me
trying to pass the B-A-R
or get a P-H-D
a dope C-A-R
and a chick that's B-A-D
in this white man's world
word to Tu-P-A-C

see, I paid for school to get a job
just to get a job so I can pay for school
getting grown
student loans
I think I let them take me for a fool

I broke into her mansion in Delaware
there's no turning back and I'm well aware

of the consequences
of robbing this chick
regardless, I'm down for whatever
catching federal charges
I came thru the 2nd story window
and then slowly got my gadgets out my trench coat
I then go
down steps pacing
thinking time is a wasting
and if I had a safe, where would it be? I guess the basement.
So I made it to a room
full of drones on the phone
calling people by first name they don't even know
they seemed caught in a trance on that side
and on the next block
others were typing letters in a sweatshop.
I saw the safe with a controller
hooked up to a desktop
I tried "money" as the password
but, I guess not
then it came through and hit me profoundly
that cash rules everything around me
I typed in "cream," then it flashed all green
and it came to a screen with a great amount
billions of dollars of debt for all the scholars
with interest so I decide to take it out
no more work like a Jamaican now
this is my move I gotta make it now
so after I erased the data
I took what was remaining
and transferred to my nonprofit bank account
I did it to give students a chance to win and grow
I wanted to give 'em grants instead of loans
somebody's gotta stand, tough
just then the Secret Service burst in
and I just put my hands up...

damn...
they finna throw me straight in a cell
I already know I'm taking an L
I end up in court with a *P.D.*, praying for help
and the judge says: "what do you have to say for yourself?"
I said...
"I paid for school to get a job
just to get a job so I can pay for school
getting grown...student loans
I think I let them take me for a fool."

#56barsofhappiness

first off, you choose to be happy or not
and lady I think your hair is beautiful, nappy or not

misery loves company so don't get trapped in that plot
just be alone or find someone that makes you happy a lot

and while you're searching
looking to eye that person
make sure you find your purpose
answers in time will certainly
start to come from deep inside of you behind a curtain
controlled by a switch that went from low to a higher circuit

and know your mind ain't worthless
it's just like fertile earth and
whatever you decide to plant in it
in due time will surface

so I can sow a dream and yield a field of fire burning ambition or
plant some mindless rhymes
and harvest tired verses
but, I'm out here hurdle stepping
for personal perfection
no speed-balling
I'm just slow and steady turtle repping

you are what you think you are
I hope you learned your lesson
you create your reality
based on your perception

and Mama told me
don't be in a hurry

only worry if you don't pray
if you gon' pray then don't worry

don't be scary
you'll be surprised at what
little faith enhances
or how GOD be making miracles
out of imperfect chances

making impossible possible
cleaning a dirty canvas
what is an obstacle?
I don't believe in circumstances!

but, I used to limit myself
to what I first was handed
in a public school system
that taught me some hurtful standards

they gave unique people the same test
if that ain't foolish
enough, they said if you don't score high,
then you won't make it thru and I know
an eagle is made to fly when the wings are in usage
but if you judge its swimming ability it'll think it's stupid

so if they say you're bad at math,
that don't mean you can't use it
you just might be better
at English, Reading or making music

you could be an eagle with wings
and not be thinking to use 'em
'cause they got you in a chicken coop
and wonder, "why he ain't producing?"

the last thing that
I want you to bite on and chew it
is to be happy
because you are living breathing and moving

fingers and ears good
I bet you're texting, listening to it
and by the end if I did a good job
then you're gonna loop it
loop it, replay it, rewind it, be reminded
find more reasons to be happy
less excuses for the whining

I know you got your struggles
but life is too short to waste time in
complaining and then
beating a horse that is already dying

my point, is if you are listening
I'm speaking to you and
don't believe in status quo
just keep on thinking you can do it

be happy put energy
and everything all up into it
whatever you want to do and
don't let your genius be ruined

say I'm gucci, I'm deso'
don't want you to bother me, so
you can keep yo'
negativity from me
go 'head and repo

I said, I'm gucci I'm deso'
don't want you to bother me, so

you can keep yo'
negativity from me
go 'head and repo
see I'm hoping to prosper
enough dough so I can cop a
seat by Oprah at the opera
or the Oscars, eating popcorn

probably Orville Reddenbacher
drinking soda, not vodka
tap her shoulder
say, "I watch M.C. on OWN
and that it's proper.

Master Class
it's provoking me to
open up my options
and be sharpened
when an opportunity just goes a knocking

I will be ready, but until that happens
I will remain a dapper, rappin', fly chappie
because I'm happy…

compton, chicago

summertime Chicago
duck behind your car door
run and hide
run inside get to safety
cause yester
or just today
these bullets get to spray
say "hi" to ya
nick or ricochet
through little Hadiya
Nick or Rick or Shay
only if they went
a different way
the preacher wouldn't get to say
R-I-P from the pulpit today
when the news reached Mama Earth
them words had her running back
words had her running backwards
she was farther in denial
tears running backwards
just like water in the Nile
screaming "Father not my child!
Father, not my child,
please don't make it harder
or make him a martyr. Not right now!"
most people heard of Oscar just right now!
and that's a whole other part of the problem just right now!
It's hot, so we're on dummy now
you get mugged when it's muggy out
slumped when it's sunny out
A/C off
and the welfare money's out
shorty's looking for her dad

so she's running out
face made, dressed up,
short shorts, tummy out
ran into buddy down the street
cause the bus is down
but his car got A/C
so she busses down
6 months later,
stomach out, baby coming now
she see buddy everyday but he running 'round,
dodging her, ducking cops
stuffing rocks, up in socks
wrong turn
up in other blocks
now he's ducking shots
reach for his waist
un-tuck a glock
bust a couple shots
with no aim
caught another child
another one to mourn
same night premature his son was born
as he was arrested
he said to me
all I heard was blue
as my mirandas were red to me.

ownership will take you far

"I never meant to…"
does absolutely nothing
for feelings post-hurt.

the son of james evans

what's the price of a black life in Florida?
that's 1500
for the son of James Evans
what's the price of a black life in Florida?
at least 10k
for funeral direction

or ...
30,000 more for the
business supporting the
prison importing the
ninjas pulling triggers
and torturing
causing coroners reporting
another killing recorded

for important
statistical digits
encouraging citizens
to shoot black on site
I mean back on site
even them athletes
that got on Nikes
damn, damn, damn, James
he's the next to go
if he don't act right
and play his Esther role.

It ain't safe, dude!
you ain't safe, too!
black boys came thru
slain in the same noose

new Strange Fruit
Gatorade-flavor-made juice
if you drank it
you'd probably hate the taste, too

you could't stomach those shots
you couldn't take it straight dude
it's bad for your liver, Fam
hard liquor
real bitter man
the cold kick will make you shiver, man
chase it with Arizona and Skittles
that's a Zimmer-
man...

fly on the wall

I be on my fly tip
looking like pilot goggles
'cause my eyes big
every now and then
I get into some boo boo
miss the trap and
other times
I standby
and watch it happen

posted on the wall
in a barber shop
people sitting in chairs
conversation sparking off
talking 'bout
getting off the block and not
serving and dropping off
just then the barber stopped

he started spraying disinfectant
cleaning off his clippers
and it made me light headed
like I'd been drinking liquor

and that stuff mess with my breathing
so instead of set there
I flew out to go get some fresh air

posted on the bricks
on the graffiti in the alley
the guy who just left the chair
was out there smiling
a customer was waiting
she just left

from dropping her granddaddy
out at Bingo
so she could go cop her some
granddaddy sour diesel

a cop noticed the transaction
let the girl leave
then approached the man asking:
"I thought you knew the drill?
you know, I'mma catch feelings
if you act brand new
and don't run me my percentage

you supposed to give me a cut of that
c'mon run it back,
run it back
what?
you ain't got?
just confess it
c'mon, answer my question!"
he said, "I want a lawyer"
the cop said, "you're under arrest" and then
they started wrestling
fighting reckless
two bullets went in a neck
and the side of a small intestine
the dealer was leaking, bruh
the cop retrieved the funds
planted rocks in his pocket
and called the people to clean him up

I saw the whole thing
but I ain't do nothing
I ain't wanna get killed
so I ain't move nothing

sorry, dope boy
I wish I could've helped you
but I'm just a fly on the wall

I saw the whole thing
but I ain't do nothing
I ain't wanna get killed
so I ain't move nothing

sorry dope boy
I wish I could've helped you
but I'm just a fly on the wall

and I be on my fly tip
lookin like pilot goggles
'cause my eyes big
every now and then
I get into some boo boo
miss the trap and
other times I standby
and watch it happen...

riches vs wealth

if he's never taught
financial literacy
he will waste fortunes.

fifty | 50

she say it's 50/50
I say, naw, you don't get me
I give you all I have
and when you pull out I feel empty
you walk around here
like you don't know your butt stank
you pushed me in the street when the bus came
took off like a Mustang
left me naked while you half-assed
I still turned the other cheek
without complain-
ing about one thang
see, cause my love ain't
cheap, and you must ain't
meet a king, only them so-called ballers that pump fake
and you jumped...hey
reaching for some-thang
now you finna crash going down a one way

so now you sit at home
just alone
wish and moan
with your home-sister
cause misery loves to kick it strong
and she listens on
when she leaves, you get your phone
drunk texting and dialing me
confessing that it was wrong
your mind's drifting on
sitting posting pictures on
instagram with a dude that looks just like me
he's just a clone
and a rebound
probably in it just to bone,

break up with you just to go to come around and get some mo'
babygirl, who told you this was Rome?
relationships should be reciprocal
very intentional
not stereotypical
or parody fictional
and no individual
living person and perfect
so there will be friction, teamwork, addition,
and some division though.
the mother of learning is repetition so,
know if you slack on your giving
you'll always be hypocritical
insecure because you know you could be giving mo'
instead of 50/50, joe.

when expectations don't meet reality
you've got a problem
this math don't add up
...50/50...
I don't want half of nothing
and you shouldn't either
it's supposed to be 100/100
that means if you're lacking
I pick up where you're slacking
you can mistake a cup for half empty
or half full
but if you give your all
you can walk away with no regrets
pissed off nonetheless
but you'll know that you've done all you could
the other person just wasn't ready to get it
in double-dutch
the rope can't swing if yo' whole body ain't in it
we gotta jump together
both risking getting whipped by the rope

but when we do
I'll lick your wounds
and you'll put honey on my cuts as we laugh
about the day we took jumping rope to another level
redefined comfort levels
joined forces and fought other devils
together
I'm not interested in 50/50
standing with one foot in
never jumping
rope steady slapping us in the arm,
leg,
neck,
head,
and we wonder why it's not working
why it's not turnin'

you don't complete me,
you compliment me
GOD ain't make no half people
I'm already 100
and so are you.

heartbreak therapy verse

she's like:
"you always got the answer, don't you?
blahzay, skip back
this that,
I bet if I was a gig, you wouldn't miss that!
and it's odd to me
that since I'm not your boss,
I can't possibly get some reciprocity."

I'm like, you mean the world to me, babe
but you don't pay my bills
so while I'm on this grind
just be patient and chill
I'm trying to make a mil'
so let's go make a meal,
eat and talk about the future, how to make a way and still

be caught in the allure
relationships take work
but they should not be a chore
much more like a perk
it took my mama and my papa
nine months to create a player
she wants a real life, video game create-a-player

love and trust
she can have all that
she still wants to condition me under the *Pavlov* act
wants me to want to do what she wants me to do
pop quiz
and think I better score a hundred and two
but that's too much to ask
I can't be giving that gist

she wants my fore-thought
and thought to have a feminine twist

I'm a male
different chromosome
just a guy
that's why my questions for your methods
come with an extra "why?"

I'm sad, I miss you
I'm done grabbing tissues
but almost all of my exes had daddy issues

and if you don't have respect for your Papa
it's hard to find respect for me, Mama

I had to say "bye-bye"

teach love, not to hit licks

brothers waste love that
sisters give freely, 'cause they
never learned value.

the makings of a dog

I heard Mama say: "all men are dogs!"
and though she don't mean that, bro,
she repeated it so much,
I started to believe that, bro.
she say: "all men are dogs!"
and though she don't mean that, bro
she repeated it so much
I started to believe that, bro.

I was too young to understand sarcasm
you couldn't tell me nothing
my mother was just as stubborn
Papa wouldn't argue with her
so she thought that he didn't love her
he got that foolishness from my Auntie,
with her single ass...

I remember it,
I was in the kitchen washing dishes
while long-distance listening
to my Mama while she sitting in the chair
getting locs twisted in her hair
and the logic that my Auntie said got
her literally twisted in her head
she was like: "In this life, love be no fair,
for these experiences there be no fare
that you can pay off with C-notes there, it's a different one.
dollars not accepted...insufficient funds.
'cause for this love learning keep in mind,
that they only take the currency of time!"
so time went on
and she got with this guy that was treating her wrong
the whole time I was peeping it
first she would speak with him

then she think she needs a man,
so now she gotta be with him
he'd take her out, treat her nice,
next thing you know, she'll sleep with him
months down the line he's keeping them eyes black
but she don't fight back
unless its right back to be with him
and I don't like that,
or the fact that she be believing him
he tells her all lies
you'd think she'd be leaving him
but nope…
instead she just watched him
cause she said 'being lonely is not an option'

but I'm young…
so instead of me reading between the lines
and seeing that my Mama's thinking needed be re-aligned
I was the example to see in time
and he was heartless,
but regardless got treated like he was prime
so with me seeing this,
you know what happened to me inside?
myself turned to me
and said that he wanted to be this guy!
mama treat him so good…
but he do her so wrong,
but she just put up with it and been through it so long
my daddy didn't do it, and she said to him: "So long!"
so I kind of think this dog dude is so "on!"

Mama said "all men are dogs!"
and though she don't mean that, bro
she repeated it so much
I started to believe that, bro
time passed and she's saying the same quote to me

so now I'm thinking this is the man I am supposed to be
so I soon replaced the word "man" with "dog"
and it didn't seem all that bad of a word to me
cause when you think about it…
"man's best friend."
"that's my dog!"
"what's up, dog?!"
who her?
well, I go and come,
but gee, I see she stays,
so if I'm a D-O-G then she's my
be, eye, tee, see, H

mama say: "all men are dogs!"
and though she don't mean that, bro
she repeated it so much
…I started to believe that, bro

'cause I got with this chick that broke my heart
and I was pissed
because I let what she did affect me so much
'cause I couldn't get back at her and be her equal
I was taught: "you gotta get them first, or it's your ego!"
I didn't learn "equa"
so I set out to make people feel how I felt
because "hurt" people hurt people!

plus my Papa, he's just a sucker
Mama didn't stay and go with him
and for whatever reason,
she wit' this homie that's bogus so I'm going in!

one of the many I was sexing I'd been knowing for years
she opened up to exposing her fears
I told her what I had to
blowing smoke in her ears

clouding her thoughts
just like dude did Moms while he was holding her rear
I said I wanted to take time off
'cause I was bored on the real
she told me: "you broke my heart"
but I'm ignoring her tears
now I got two more girls, then four
switching a different pair
of women
doing mental damage
but, man I didn't care
wash, rinse, and repeat after I spill out the plan
more random sex to temporarily feel like a man
'cause when I tell guys
they respond positive and make me feel like "The Man"
even thought after I'm done coming
I feel like a young dummy
that's horny
and less of a man than I am when I'm telling that story

the last woman that dated me
she told me she took a chance
'cause she wasn't
believing the hype
nor did she care
that my reputation preceded me
but when she left
she told me that she needed me
to understand that she would not
be dogged and mistreated so she was leaving me
I waited for her to call me a "dog"
but in the last of her speech to me
she said she wouldn't
because somebody had just mislead-ed me
and these quotes echoed and repeatedly
played in my head

like an indecisive hair-cutter's hand
without his barber license
for slicing a near 'nother strand

yeah, brother man
it's deeper than just "macking" right
she said I wasn't acting right
and that "DOG" word just described what I was acting like
but it don't make me that
just 'cause of what my actions is
it's just a slang, far-fetched noun posing as an adjective
taken out of context and given another definition
and spoke and said thru this "mother of learning" in repetition...

"all men are dogs!"
...and though she don't mean that, bro
she repeated it so much,
I started to believe that, bro
so what?
now you're saying that I'm crazy
you're saying this is how I'm not supposed to treat a lady
you're saying this is how I'm not supposed to be behaving
well before you take that critic seat and proceed to degrade me
remember you haven't seen what I seen
and didn't raise me...

rape culture gene pool

by ~~encouraging~~ programming a young man
to chase after vagina,
you are indirectly
teaching disrespect
for the ~~gender~~ woman it belongs to

sexual miseducation

It's all a fallacy
I think I'm outta touch with reality
I was taught that it was okay to casually
have sex
as long as I got a strap with me
but at what point does "casually" become "rapidly"
and the next thing I know
my manhood and sexuality
becomes based on sexing until it's all outta me!
what if you just keep wasting your seeds
and one day they just run out?
billions of children
buried and twisted up
in latex body bags all so you can get a nut
don't get me wrong, sex is great when you can get it up
but tell me when is enough been enough?
so many loose ends and soul-ties
taking orders from this head that you're pissing from
got you ending up
revisiting relationships and thus
some of us want to get in "-nupts"
excuse me, get in nuptials
and we be the gender wondering why women be rushing you
you're crazy thinking it's a lot that women want from you,
but all they want is you;
which isn't much
but it seems like a lot because you always give it up
you give away a different piece
every time that you get some cut
so when you go to turn in your player card
for your ring finger "wrist-a-cuffs"
you're missing stuff!

confessions of a satyromaniac

I wasn't addicted to the vagina
I was addicted to the whining
addicted to the mental pictures of love-faces
night visions of different positions and cum-placing
I became complacent
with giving women my shoes to live in with soul laces
I'm thinking it's so basic
not knowing that every time I hit the twat
I'm soul-tying double and triple knots
we talk big a lot
the idea of no strings attached is a slick premise
but the reality of it all is fictitious
it isn't ever right
or ever clever to sever ties
and think you'll lose a part of you never
and have a better life

if you triple knot a shoe
when you go to untangle it
in the process you risk getting it tangled again
especially if you go fast
so you gotta take your time
or you can just cut it off
and lose a part of it
that is... a part of yourself
in the process.

closed hands drop touchdown passes

she loves all of him,
but he don't love him, so he
misunderstands her.

the death of hip-hop

somehow it seems like we got away from the elements
it's about the dollars
so the knowledge is all irrelevant
I'll translate it in layman's or eloquent
labels don't care about your talent excelling
if you ain't selling it!

they wanna see platinum
and to see paper stacking
less about MC-ing, DJ-ing, B-Boy-ing and tagging
culture verses industry
industry and culture
industry don't keep it real
culture is supposed to

and some of this new food for thought
gives me an ulcer
as soon as it comes out on the shelf,
I be like "no sir"
it's like hip-hop got in bed with industry
and he stroked her
bent her over
pimped her, hoed her,

sold her back to the Blacks with nothing on
young mind, fronting grown
getting her Benjamin Button on
now baby lies in the hospital on her backside
heart beats: "Boom…Bap"
and it flatlines.

outkast intro:

outkast
to outlast
2 decades
without trash
they blasted off out past
Earth to planet Stankonia and now back
to give you
these once mastered hits
remix you
with DJ Cutmaster Swiff
he brought it back

rolled up fat and lit
this Outkastic spliff
to Puff, pass and switch
(record scratch)
Puff pass and switch
I don't even know what's after this
for 20 years
they kept you
jammin' in yo socks
pajamas and flip flops
reppin' West Savannah and The SWATs
Atlanta, 1st generation Dungeon Family is not
about calamity
'less you trying to damage in they spot

They ain't havin' that
the 2 dope boyz in a Cadillac
. . . everlasting
matta' fact, you ain't gotta act
all different like they ain't two of the illest, realest spittin' it
south of the Mason-Dixon line
and eastward of the Missisip'

yes yes y'all, all of you should come to get with this
literary league of extraordinary gentlemen
Possum Alouishus Jenkins
and Francis the Savannah Chittlin' Pimp,
yes look!
Dookie Blossom Gang the 3rd
and Sir Lucious Left Foot
Funk Crusader, Love Pusher
Daddy Fat Sax
Billy Ocean
got that?
Big Boi and André 3000
that's stacks!

It's so necessary, so relevant
one DJ, 2 fellas with
intelligence,
too effortless,
timeless lyrics with new messages
soul food for thought
Hootie Hoo!
blessing it
on the house, so you don't have to pay though
from fish and grits to
beats and mashed potatoes
they know that it's fire and finger-licking
and rather delicious
cause you're already listening and I say so.
Aye, joe!

offspring of public schooling

communication be 90%
nonverbal to me though
that why only ten percent of text messages
mean what they mean so
the other ninety percent
of what you're typing to say
escapes all meaning
and goes out on vacation
that's what happens when you
lose tone of voice
inflection and pacing,
speed, delivery, diction and articulation

aha! now I see why *Word*
first had spell check
and then evolved to grammar faster
because those people that were not
spelling bee clever masters
depended on the word processor
to basically auto-edit half or
more of their term papers to get an "A"
and live happily ever after

cutting corners
c'mon people!
we forgot the mission
answers are no longer fill-in-the-blank
that's why teachers be teaching reading comprehension
they wouldn't have to create more classes
called "We Forgot to Mention"
but that's what happens when
you choose speed and not precision

I mean as a child
if you give me a test with 4 answers to pick from
I'm not reading the entire chapter
for the assignment that you sent, Bruh!
that's y'all fault!
once upon a time

someone got lazy
I mean innovative
and said I spend way too much time
with these papers that I'm grading
I don't know about you, Dog
but it's minimizing the time spent with children
and I don't like my ears chewed off
by my wife
so I have to come up with a way
to teach lessons
and grade 'em too, Dog!

eureka!
I'll create an answer key
grade all at once
not knowing that in the future
those children would grow up
12 years of learning there's only one answer
while obtaining the knowledge
now you wonder why they can't
choose a major in college?

then when the system chews and spits them out
they become the top drinkers
cause you taught them to be
workers and not thinkers.
so they can't understand
while they're offspring
don't want to be workers
and never want to be not dreamers
double negative
that came out positive
aww Jesus!

why do these young'ns dream too much?
because CEOs and inventors
think too much.
and we learned about them in school,
no you
or any chapter about
Mr. & Mrs. Always Did I Was Told To.

a perfect her

I love melanated women
with large lexicons
100% female
please no Decepticons
she gotta read books
must love what grows out her scalp
and yeah, wear her hair
know the difference between
there, their, and they're

impeccable hygiene
rolls with the punches
and the struggle through life
very classy
Claire Huxtable-like
innovative, DIY creative
you know the usual
I should be able to close my eyes and
still tell that she's beautiful
character and spirit
overlooks looks
physical beauty fades
but that personality
way of thinking and living remains
so I gotta ask myself
if I were to conceive a child
with the next woman that I lay
and worst case scenario
GOD forbid that
s/he takes me away
and the boy or girl
twins or triplets
were nurtured everyday
by their mother
and grew to be just like her
would I be okay
with that?
think about it
would I wanna play with that?

nope.
sidenote
quit playing
go head delete your Tinder, fam
get your life together
less than 60 days
before November, fam

carbondale coffee

online
checking my email
when I got a letter from
MC at the Source Magazine
that said
'say Black,
please send high resolution
photos of you ASAP.'
I think I sent them a link
way back in July
with a template
press release about
The Mo' Better Mixtape
mixed by Sean Ace
and produced by Authentik Made

I had a few beats blessed on
by Matcy P, Chris Mathien and Choice Teflon
potent rhyming dope
never been stepped on
with baby laxative
no lazy accidental
angry at the mental
only crazy paper rapping scribbles
wordplay and multi-page
syllabic riddles
flowing at beginning
mixed with syncopation at the middle
raw and unpolished at the least
well, maybe at the little

I had also written
a hip hop musical
minus the usual
instrumentation accompany
only a'capella moving you
called The Yard
I promoted for a hard month
sat in the student center every day

next to Starbucks
like I got them tickets
I got them tickets, joe
don't wanna miss it
don't wanna miss it, no
from 9am to 4pm I would post,

let the people know
then after four
I would go to Kampus Kuts
check my emails and verse through
some new rhymes
until it was time for rehearsal
at Quigley Auditorium
although this was history in the making
I am no historian
just a time traveller
born two years after '84
with no DeLorean

after that
go to a local event
and or
get something to eat
from Don Taco
and then before I go to sleep

watch documentaries and battle rap
text and Facebook
you and your friends
wake up around 8:30am
and do it again.

advice to a younger me

dear Moodah Man aka Iceberg
let me put you on game for this life sir
don't fall for every girl
just because you like her
you shouldn't have given shorty your Gameboy pro'ly bruh
when she dropped you and kept it
I know you was salty, huh?

Don't surprise old girl if you ain't official
that'll save you some heartbreak
slow jam CDs skipping and hella tissue

around 5th grade
there'll be a sweetheart
moving from Mississippi
she'll know what time it is
she'll teach you black is beautiful
and spark your confidence

and homie I know you got a thing
for the hoodrats
your scary self should've actually chose one,
fell in love and never looked back.

don't be scared to be yourself
don't be scared to be yourself
don't swing on Miss Hickman
you'll never connect and
reckless ain't your lifestyle
I hope you get the message

thank your friends Mr. Wilburn and Morris,
your old Gus Macker partners
for calming you down and dragging you to the office
thank your Papa
for not beating you like you stole something
keeping his promise
he was like
go to school, go home

go nowhere else
keep on your grind
and if you act up again
I'll pop up at school and beat your behind
in front of your peers
so they know that I love you
and that Donald Leroy Williams Jr.
don't take no mess
or no trouble

when you get to high school
stay involved, joe
don't be average
do your personal best
and stand tall, joe
keep bringing that radio before school
but jump in the cypher this time
you're kinda raw, joe
tell Corey Simmons
don't quit spitting he got bars, joe
and it's okay to look up to
Tron, Mark-Todd & Kamal, joe
if you see Brandon McKissick
tell him you're his biggest hooper fan
and he's like the AND1 basketball Superman star, joe
when you get to SIU
don't break no hearts, joe
cause someone will mysteriously
break your car, joe
it just stopped running out the blue
that's lowkey a pun
if you know me or got a clue
inside jokes with me & the crew

don't open the door for shorty
that's looking for Earl
and leave that Queen alone
quit being selfish
you know she loves you
don't mess with other girls

keep it real when she asks you
she lowkey already know
your behavior and how you are
she just wanna show
you the benefit of the doubt
and see if you wanna grow
don't be dishonest
that's a character flaw
she's gonna go!

learn martial arts, wrestling,
time and respect
if you see someone talking
out the side of they neck
to any black sister
not just your sister
give them a check
don't put your hands on them
but get their perspective

slanted right
never take your words
for granted like
what I got to say ain't important
this is GOD planning right?
I Am gave you a gift
to move with a movement
so sharpen your skill set
use it or lose it!

braggadocio

September 17th
heavenly
cleverly
tethering
wordplay
heard they
common hating
worst way
First Take
ESPN
commentating
instigate this
single man
Mr. Bay-less
lonely people
only Beatles repeated
metaphor envy
Eleanor Rigby
nifty clips
violin nice clean
1966
had a tight dream
I delivered triplet sons
calling grandma
to the woman that had me
my skills grew on them gladly
my son say that's overkill
you ain't gotta prove to them daddy
they just
say your bars are Stephen A. Smith
they think you're Ludacris' daddy!
hold up
you're doing 'em badly
slow down
I think you losing 'em
like maneuvering switching
UBERs and taxis
using the app too and dispatching
cruising thru

passing beautiful
new to you designed Subarus laughing,
like, who'd have knew
someone with a computer to actually
develop over and over
a model one or two and then have to
draft it
after
craft it
pack it
fast with
matte and plastic
glass and
pass it
choose it
check it
thru inspection
prove it
cruise it
through the
checklist
tighten brakes
press the center and
license plate
on the fender man
fire rhymes
byproduct
is embers and
ampersand...

September fourteenth
a case of the Mondays
can render cubicle
workers crazy
raging for gunplay
patience can and will often break
if you disrespect the Swingline
stapler of the staple
in the office space
he's been here forever
this is a freestyle write

every now & again
I can be loud hype
don't label me
or box me in
you can't keep wildlife
but some sisters' vibes
demand an attraction with him
and this true MCs
flammable active rhythm
is basically animal magnetism
no ghost-writing here
or tangible apparition
from a mechanical rap division
contacted by
summoning candles to that dimension
for deceased lyricist spiritual
channeling smoking
botanical cannabis after vision

sober mind
this is flowery jargon
showing I'm
more than capable
of holding my
own when goes to fine
art written as
a contemporary form of literature
spoken rhyme
no explanation
this is
Sierra Leone
land purchasing
diamond excavation owner
just know that the flow is mine!
braggadocio declines

baggage claim

when it comes to relationships
trust is a must
too grown for you to be paranoid running amok
asking me
to go thru my phone
two grown people
too grown for me
to be looking thru your phone equal
that's lame fronting
while I'm stunting
besides the brain can and will
make something out of nothing

and that's the truth about dishonesty
if you honor me
you'll let me be
before you funnel out the hate
looking funny at the face
insecure and paranoid
cause you didn't check
your duffel at the gate
before we boarded
down sat
seat bucked and stowed our trays

and a gentlemen is never to be petty tit-for-tat
open doors and carry bags too
but we give them back

like this is yours!
here you have it
here's your luggage
I mean your baggage
kinda heavy
I see the shoulder lean and sagging
that ain't supposed to be
how long have you had it?
will I help you unpack it?
sure, but while we're acting cordial

understand I can't unpack it for you
I did that before too
thinking I was helping purposely
because shorty in Texas told me help
all this extra weight was hurting me
and I'm a problem solver
so I took initiative and unpacked it all
with courtesy
but when it wasn't working she needed to repack
dip and hurdle me
she got all confused and accused me
of burglary!
that was the end of story
choosing hard at hookah bars
she never took inventory
lookin' like goofy mark
from Goofy Park
pointing fingers like
you took this from me!
nope I didn't grab it.
I'm missing some other stuff too!

Nope, didn't even know you had it!
now she at a new location
not enjoying her destination
cause she contacting
Delta Airlines every day and
asking for replacement items
and when she get back home
and hesitates to go or come or not
new experience is wack
'cause emotions were in another spot
life is too short
can't be kicking punts
you only get one
and you can only spend it once
tall or small, big or short
bank amount
leave it in or take it out
make sure you make it count

respect the dj

for the 919
and the 336
when the nighttime comes
that's how we do this

got that from Little Brother
Phontigallo
of Greensboro, NC
yeah he be spitting some of
that realness along with grade A
wordplay it isn't none of
anything short of true MC-ing
no spitting covers
only original instrumental lovers
of the producer member, Wonder
9th Wonder
and until now it didn't dawn
on me like my twin sister
from a different mother

that he was the DJ of the group
as well as producer playing them too
all respect to the disk jockey
hip hop gets sloppy when they act in here
and promote the walk-thru person
and not the one that controls the atmosphere

backwards yeah
like putting the carriage before the horse
that be all bad
backwards like S-D raw kcab
backwards like having candles
and burning them during the day outside
when your power's cut off
and you have to gamble
backwards like racecar in reverse
wait, that's a bad example

back to the subject

DJs started the party beginning
when playing vinyl records
non-stop and then mixing
MCs wasn't rapping then
they were just on the mic
getting the crowd hype
making them clap a hand

or two and wave them in the air
while B-Boys were waiting to jump in
at the part where the lyrics ended
and instrumentation
would come in

graffiti artists were tagging something on the walls
just like Egyptians might have did with hieroglyphics
fast-forward
hip-hop sold units in higher digits
and labels signed artists thinking they didn't require mentions
of language including DJs
within the finer imprint
and some took it on the chin
diminished title within
some groups were like 'nah
this is my crew, if he don't get it,
then I ain't with it'
others were like 'just hire me
on the tour and I'mma fit him in.

2015 and the club scene is different
partygoers go to text on their phone
not to even witness
the talents of the DJ cutting, mixing and fever switching
all while having a good time and get a little fitness.

knowing this
it should change
but new guys undercut
and promoters throw a fit
when you mention pricing
they act like you're not that important then

they place a price on
atmosphere transformation, energy flow
and since they forget
I just tell them what you pay for is what you're gonna get

and in your own defense
I know your funds maybe low
and I get it cause I understand broke
but lowkey, no offense
if the funds are really that short
then I reckon' you shouldn't throw events
if you want to hire a DJ
but your budget cannot hold expense
pay what they want
or choose a different person
good or bad the people won't forget
and keep in mind that
without a DJ the party don't exist!

everybody eats, b!

blessed to know
several artists of all
locations and directions
no slouches
all of them respect us
and how we approach our talents
ask me for suggestions
I'll recommend
some iron that sharpens iron
I'll gladly be the nexus

I'll share the wealth
Hater-ation is forever always weak, G
'cause how I see it
everybody eats, B!

I want everyone to win
money can't compare to joy
plus, if I'm at the top by myself, then I'm paranoid
I don't have respect for myself
if I'm trying to keep another brother down
I'm not checking myself
I first invest in myself
then pay forward opportunity
not think less of myself
eventually
employ my brother
so he can restart the cycle
and start to write some checks to himself
then invest in himself
wash, rinse repeat
wash rinse repeat
dodge, miss, defeat

I say this to prove to most of you
that I never wanna rule over you
ain't no fun in that
yes, player
I usually take care of my lady when she under the weather

but in this case,
no time for bae sick
I'mma chess player!

I did that just to show how far petty wordplay can make a statement
stretch layers
subject changed back
check, player
your move...

the law of nature

dear black woman,
I love the way you love
how you're oh so passionate
I promise to love me more
so I can love you more accurate

I know you're disappointed
in the way I treat me
because the way I treat thee
has been a repeat
gimme three feet

it's in my nature
to protect a family and bring home bacon

and it's your nature to
comfort show love and affection greater

but when you're taught to wear your feelings
on sleeves and remain adjacent
we run into a problem
when reality don't meet expectations

because in the barbershop
It's regarded hot
to have multiple women thinking they are the one
we all are taught

the blind leading the blind & deaf
we all are not
listening
some brothers think they're supposed be pimping
until they get a balding spot

so we grow up
leaving the other stranded
and she taught to be the bigger person
creating a double standard
at first sight

love took flight but trouble landed
she was supposed to get a fair turn
but he was double-handed
she declared a misdeal
she say 'I don't play that way
high ace is it!
you play with jokers, boy
that there be 15 spades
that don't make no sense

they agree to disagree
so nobody ain't gon get
what they want,
they both know better
but the law of nature says, "don't quit!"

for grandma noodie

wrote this while texting and driving
on my way to DJ a wedding celebration of triumph
reception uniting
black love progression and tying
the knot
trying to not be an emotional wreck but I'm crying
snot dripping
spilling tears reflecting the life of
the matriarch on my Mama's section and side of
the family
when I heard this beat, her spirit crept up inside me
and I said 'hello, Grandmama,
man I thought you would live forever, decided
you'd be centuries like them folks you said were blessed in the bible
it was only so many years left and I tried to
visit more, but it was hard to witness your health start declining
heaven gave us an angel from the shelf of designer
queens with a little extra love left up inside her
I met GOD and she's black
all facts
everything I had heard
she personified in words

she was a hardcore
no nonsense
5'6"
clean, queen goddess
with a conscience
never ever, ever, ever,
spoke without content
worked for the post office
39 years,
no problems
it was gold to see her crack a smile
a faithful member of the Broadview Baptist choir
attended every Sunday
offering? she gotta tithe!
always paid her tax on time
respectable, never tats on thighs

seems like I was just taking her to the store
in my Papa's Cadillac
opening doors
wishing security would
say something about me
chauffeuring my Mama's mama
Grandma Noodie aka Lois E.
a black woman
that woman
that'll love you and cook a fire meal
after delivering ass whoopins
then fix her roof and put shingles up in the heat
big mamas like this are becoming extinct!

just over broke

700 a month
for a townhouse back in college
in the Chi, that won't even get you a closet
so now I'm back at the next
Momskillet and Pops and I guess
I can't have honeys over
to stroke, cuddle and mack
only growth
with operation: 'hope, hustle and stack!'
I'm so lowkey
so under the mat
cutting grass, washing dishes and errand-running for snacks
career hunting for a grind to strive
but I'm too talented to work a nine-to-five
eight-to-four
or ten-to-six
that's a whole third of my day when I begin the shift

and add another hour
for travel to and from the office or tower
warehouse
department store
sweatshop
factory
I had to quit all that
all that as wack to me
code switching for supervisors and faculty
using ten percent of my brain
taking my black from me
suited and booted in my trench overcoat
to work a J-O-B
and be just over broke.

parenting advice from a former child

if you teach a child fear, they won't respect you.

teach them integrity.

replace:
"don't do that because you'll get caught"

with:
"don't do that because it's not the right thing to do"

love totaled

I met GOD
she taught me love
right after I broke her heart

    that's all she knew

        she found it important that I learn the skillset
        because the alternate school of thought
        that taught me
        missed a few steps

    there I was...

driving on the left side
of a two-way street in Illinois
after crashing into her
and damn near totaling her car
she forgave me
and directed me to the right side.

        she said she was going to get her car repaired
      and didn't want me to hit anyone else on my journey.

love = verb

Love has *always* been a verb.

 once folks started trying to make it a noun,

 it became difficult.

new revolution verse

in a country that is capitalistic
the poor folks
labeled 'capital misfits'
some can't afford a cap on a lipstick
or to pay attention
so they ask for assistance
Uncle Sam say: 'before we proceed,
Mama gotta kick Daddy out to receive green.'
laughing like: 'Hee! Hee! Hee!
she thinks they're out of debt
'cause I took out the D,
and left her with E-B-T.'

she said ain't nothing wrong with money, that is a tool
of use, it's the love of money that is the root
of evil
that grew into a tree producing Z-Quill
gotta be asleep
to live an American dream still
I be the hypochondriac insomniac
balancing health and wealth
'cause I've always known where Daddy and Mommy at
plus I know where GOD be at
and know my nose
looks just like the one missing off the Sphinx
everybody eats, B!
you should've grew something
don't just stand there, do something!
I been quit saying hello to underdressed fellows
that drink only Mello Yello
'cause they come plain and do nothing.

big business

Uncle Sam wanted land on the Southside of Chicago
but the man that owned the land
would not let him buy,
so...
Uncle Sam hit up the local crooked cops
the ones that took the block
after they learn who cooks the rock
and raid the local cooking spot
slash bachelor pad
they keep half of the cash
report half of the stash
and put the rest back on the ave

meanwhile,
kids dropout and pack-sling
end up on the news
while some use and turn to crack fiends
violence multiplies
and we only seem to focus open eyes
and notice when someone older dies

the neighborhood is getting badder to manage
and uncle Sam is like:
"meh, collateral damage"

the residents don't feel safe and decide to move away
because even the local paper reads:
"It could be you today!"

now the man's land is where the killers lay
his real estate
is where the dealers stay
post up in fresh whips with dealer plates

they know if you're real or fake
by hand daps and guerilla shakes
and they spend all day
pitching to home for food on dinner plates

after that, the man's land ain't good
the value goes down
and it's a brand new hood

but, since it's close to downtown
best believe Uncle Sam
gonna come back 'round

cop it for the cheap
price it really steep
kick out the poor
call the same police

and they say to the peeps:
"please leave, don't make my weapon spray!
the new owner here
is knocking down these section 8's!"

they tell the thugs
"go back where you was hustling at!
either that
or get a bullet from a gun in your back.

make your choice,
heed this, I'm warning ya'
or get shipped to 26th and California

they want to repeat this
until the poor is out the city
and there's's only rich folk,
acting all saddity

then with a blink of his left eye
he said, "good day,
I have some business to attend to on the Westside."

manifesto

reflecting on the presents of the present
that currently add to my progression
and purposely stack up a collection
of thoughts I used to get pennies for after retrospectives
I used to slack in my profession
taking my talent for granted with no discretion
granted, I know it's a blessing
nothing to destroy
I'm a vessel for the message
and for others to enjoy

and although it will get me dough
I don't make music for them picky folks
I'm scripting a manuscript and they're writing sticky notes
I think I am dreaming
somebody pinch me bro
It went from SIU
moving out couch to couch landing
to see me stranded down & out
to outstanding
and ouch dammit
It hurts thinking about
managing being without
panicking deeper in doubt
handling heartbreaking
and on-leading
ladies for wrong reasons
selfishly wrong-deeding
on many a long evening
that was the old me and
I'm not with the score-keeping
but I got a life with more meaning
gettin' by on my grind
changing the world
reaching one rhyme at a time
black man with a plan
getting by on my grind
changing the world
reaching one rhyme at a time.

acknowledgements

Superman: I've always wanted to be like you, exactly, and go wherever you went. Through the good and bad decisions, I still look up to you. I love you.

Momskillet and Pops: Thank you both for encouraging my artistry and not demanding me (post-college) to get a job at a modern-day plantation. Y'all didn't raise a fool and you knew that. I'm glad it all worked out. – Moodah Man

Steve and Kris: Thank you for playing OutKast in the basement.

G.Dub: Thank you for playing Busta and Tribe in the Mustang.

The Chicago poetry scene: Thank you for teaching me artist etiquette, respect for the art, stage presence and giving me the skill set to rock any noisy or quiet crowd whether it's two or two hundred.

A.D. The Great: Thank you for teaching me how to access the literary world as an MC.

Karega: Peace King, I admire your integrity. You encourage me to be a better man. You are an honorable brother. I love you.

Authentik Made: You are the greatest musician, producer and vocalist that I've ever met. I'd bet the house on you any day. Nobody can hang with you. You are my brother. I love you.

Bee: Thank you for being such a selfless individual and SUPER DUPER supportive sis. I love you. Never change.

Publicist Witt: Thank you for having great taste, helping me jumpstart my indie artist career and for helping me to get settled in Atlanta.

Killer Mike: A true king. I appreciate you keeping your word. Gratitude for the verse and for asking me that one day in Stankonia, "What do you care about?"

Hypemaster Lo: I am grateful for your friendship, wisdom and shared connections.

Cutmaster Swiff: Thanks for showing a random rapping-ass stranger love.

Big Boi: True MC. Thank you for the words of encouragement and opportunity to go on tour.

André 3000: Stackz, Thank you for thinking outside of the box, for being a dope human being, for the emails and for the musical advice and compliments.

Ray Murray: Yodah! Thank you for the beats and for saying "stop talking to rappers on your songs!"

DJ Toomp: Big dawg! Thank you for believing in my vision, the dope conversations and the life advice.

J. Ivy: Your showmanship is remarkable. Thank you for setting an example.

Black Ice: I'm not coming to the money church Lol! Thank you for being such a lyrical craftsman. *Jedi bow*

Nonviolent Nonviolent: Thank you for the various jedi convos.

Underground Arts: Thank you for being the representative for poetry and hip-hop on campus.

The Yard: Thank you for believing in my vision.

M'Reld: Sis, you've taught me a lot about stage presence.

Mathien: You're incredible man. Never stop creating. Ever.

Everyone who let me crash at their spot and/or came through in the clutch: Thank you. Your generosity was not in vain. You are a part of the "Forever VIP club." When I blow-up-tuate, you'll already be on the list when I come to your city.

JC: I admire your grind big bro.

Droopy: Thanks for showing me around DC.

DC Soror Goldilocs from Connecticut: That futon was clutch. I am forever thankful.

Harold McGhee: Fam, thank you for the airbed, floor to sleep on and transportation.

Core: I admire your passion and integrity and thank you for the nickname

Sean Ace: Family bam, dookup yop for dem vox Lol. I love you bro. Thank you for everything.

X: Thanks for introducing me to the Midwest poetry circuit.

Killa: Ace, Thank you for always being there. Even with obligations.

Oracle: Ace, You personify friendship and love hard. I admire your courage.

Milton: Ace, keep making dope moves in life!

Professor Kreher: You never gave up on me and always had amazing wit. Thank you for being a dope human being.

T.T.: You are a great example of a black woman's love.

Bidman: You CAN do ANYTHING you put your mind to.

Attorney Jenkins: More big fish to come.

C. Reed: Thank you for the conversational chess, support and critical thinking challenges.

Royce: Never stop playing with 'em.

Murph: Give suckas no shine.

Pastor Phil Jackson: You are the greatest example that I've seen of a black man walking in his faith. Thank you for walking the talk.

Stevie and Elise: You are powerful and talented. Keep writing and singing. Never stop. Promise?

Felicia: Take care of my brother.

Chris Wiley: Breh…thank you for showing love and curating dope platforms for poets.

Nom: My brother, you are in the dictionary next to the word MC. Thank you for the gems.

Kamal B: You're an incredible role model. Keep excelling.

Kamal G: Remarkable work ethic. Keep spreading doughnut love.

My proofreading team: Thank you for helping! If there's still typos in here, it's my fault!

gofundme contributors

Taboo Abyss
Delisa Aldridge
Dela Amekporfor
Brittany Barrion
Candace Breedlove
Brooke Brown
Will Brown
LaTisha Bullock
Kenva Calloway
Dawnai Carson
Ariande Chambers
LaKeisha Conwell
Beth Crabtree
Kwabena Cross
Jonquil Curry
Justin Douglas
Tyson Ewing
Joven Fuego
Lori Goodar
Jan Gray
Chanell H.
Vauhnisha Holmes
T. Nicole Horne
Josefa Infante
David Jarecki
AJae Key
Adam Levin
Kaliah Liggons
Akisha Lockhart
Christal Luster
Shayna Marie
Adam Nicholson
Laquiesha Norwood
Lola Ogunnaike
Sheena Palmer

Lyrical Paradigm
Ashley Payne
Joe Picco
Jennet Posey
Janevieair Ray
Jasmine Scott
Desirée Sheppard
Kia Smith
Alana Summerville
Dominique Terry
Sherry Trotter
Amanda White
Marlo White
Caitlin Williams
G. Dianne Williams
Naamonde Williams
Rachel Williams
Anitra Wyatt
Kiara Wyatt
Karen Yarbrough

Born in Maywood, Illinois and raised in Peoria, Illinois, Brandon "Real T@lk" Williams is changing the world one rhyme at a time. Williams has toured with *Big Boi* on his "Shoes For Running World Tour" with co-headliner *Killer Mike* and has performed as a part of the ensemble *"Quincy Jones presents Lee England Jr."* He was crowned "Unsigned Hype" in the December 2009 issue of *The Source Magazine*, featured twice on *Russell Simmons's All Def Poetry* and has previously collaborated with several brands from *The New Era Cap Company* to *Verizon Wireless*. He is most recently producing his sixth album, giving guest lectures, crafting his second stage play and publishing his second piece of literary work in the form of a cookbook. He is truly a mother-loving genius, cunning linguist. His lyrics will make your brain smile. Discover more on his website, **ModernDayGriot.net**

Made in the USA
Middletown, DE
28 October 2022

13650331R00090